MONOLOGUES
FROM
MOLIERE

Selected, Edited, and Rendered
into English prose
by
Dick Dotterer

Moliere is the great man alive on stage. He is more
than a genius. He is a great soul who exhibits
himself and sacrifices himself for the theatre.

...Jacques Copeau

NOTE: "Monologues From Moliere" may be utilized for workshop, audition, special reading, and class work purposes without royalty consideration. If, however, they are presented either individually, or in total, before an audience where admission is charged, royalty payment is required. Contact publisher for applicable rates.

Dramaline Publications, 10470 Riverside Drive, Suite #201, Toulca Lake, CA 91602. 818/985-9148.

CONTENTS

Dedication

To Dr. Walther R. Volbach, who did not introduce me to Moliere, but did introduce me to many other aspects of European theatre.

INTRODUCTION
— Acting Moliere —

John Gielgud is quoted as saying that style is knowing what play you are in. If style can be defined, it must make reference to the evocation of a time, a place, and a kind of society. Much depends on physical things, as well as psychological orientation, in realizing style. The way one sits, the way one moves, the way one handles physical objects are all tied to the "external style" of the play, just as the actor's knowledge of the social, moral, and religious milieux and rituals of the period add to the emotional and psychological "internal style" of the play. Ultimately, style rests in the text of the play. Do not substitute anything else for style: style expresses what is underneath the form.

Moliere wrote at a time when France was exerting its greatest influence in Europe. He also wrote at a time when France overtly quested for elegance and refinement. He wrote at a time when a model of classical simplicity was sought in all things, and it appears to have influenced society in all things except costume, which, in spite of all efforts to discipline design, refused to surrender to simplicity. Moliere wrote in an age when behavior was so dictated that the placement of handkerchiefs in clothing indicated social position and status; when fans were used not in the conventional means, but for pointing and punctuation; when hats were worn by everyone and there was a precise etiquette for hats, including the dictum that the inside of the hat was never seen; an age when wigs were objects of competition; when there was a complete etiquette for chairs, and grave questions of precedence might arise in offering someone a chair or placement of when and where they sat. It was a time, in many ways, of exaggerated and insincere politeness. It was a time of facade and form as much as substance. To perform Moliere, an actor must know the world in which the dramatist lived, for no writer is associated more closely with the age of Louis XIV than is Moliere. An actor clarifies for an audience the historical pressures which dictate a character's behavior and relationships through manners and movement.

Also to act Moliere, one needs to know something about 17th century French theatre, both the theoretical theatre and the physical theatre and stage, as well as the conventions of both. The 17th century was known as the "Neo-Classical Period," based on a misguided and misinterpreted view of the conventions and writings of the ancient Greek and Roman Classical writers of drama and verse. Verse was reserved for heroic tragedy, and the acting style of the tragic actor was exaggerated and bombastic. Comedy was always written in prose, and farce, that low form of comedy—that "guilty pleasure"—was really the theatre meant for the peasants of the fair grounds (of course, in France's long tradition of farce a lot of noble and gentry, including the King, found themselves gravitating again and again to this form of popular theatre).

Then along came Moliere. While Moliere stayed within the conventions of the theatre in which he worked and succeeded (it never would have occurred to him to break the established rules of his theatre), he did experiment within the rules and he stretched the boundaries of his theatre to establish new forms of comedy and to raise farce and comedy of manners to distinguished art forms.

While Moliere's acting was still stylized by today's measures, it was far more realistic to the audience of his day than that of his rivals. Soon, his influence superseded others, and he came to be regarded as the finest actor of his age and the mentor of the finest actor of the next generation, Michel Baron. Moliere had the audacity to write *in verse* (the effrontery of the comedian! said the tragedians). And very good verse and poetry it was, too. He also introduced philosophical and moral questions into themes in French comedic theatre. He took stock characters from French farce and the Italian *commedia dell'arte* and gave them souls. Moliere single-handedly raised French farce from a diversion at country fairs to a distinguished and honorable comedic art form which is still a world-wide model of excellence and achievement.

The theatre of 17th century France is not one of a lot of physical movement, or one that requires a lot of necessary props and/or furniture. It has be referred to as a "stand up and talk theatre." And this quip is not too far off the mark. The dramatic action of 17th century French theatre is in the language. And this is true whether the play be by Racine or by Moliere.

Moliere's language *is* the action of his plays. He uses words to achieve a purpose. An actor needs to know the full connotations of each word in a speech to convey that particular thought. The actor must be aware of how to use his vocal instrument to orchestrate the various vocal levels the speeches of the play demand. The actor of classics must be a vocal athlete. The words demand that the actor know how to hurl them, project them, to hundreds of spectators. The actor's instrument, poorly trained and poorly exercised, will not be strong enough, supple enough, subtle enough, to enable him to express what he wants to express. The actor's mind must click with rapidity as he speaks. The actor must be absolutely clear in his mind as to what he is saying every moment of the play. There is no time to wait for inspiration and for "the right mood" to come.

To play Moliere an actor needs both constant voice training and movement training. The very long speeches in Moliere have to have changes in thought direction (afterthoughts, sub-thoughts, and even "subtext"). The tempos, the vocal pitches, and the rhythms of the speeches have to be orchestrated. The actor needs to rehearse and to work at great length on sitting and posture, on bows and curtsies, on walking and physical stance (especially men, when it comes to mastering the high-heeled shoes of the period), of the use of plumed hats and the tall walking sticks. An actor must be aware of what he is doing every moment in the play, in his role, both in rehearsal and in performance.

Because of the physical conditions and conventions of Moliere's stage, a presentational style of acting resulted. In Moliere the actor does not so much play *to* other actors as *at* them, and the actor is *always* aware of the audience out front. The sense of the speech must always come first. Moliere's writing is not realistic, and neither is the type of acting needed to play it. Both are *stylized*. Both must be played *bigger* than life, but the playing must begin with the meaning of the text. This stylization and presentational form in performing Moliere should be emulated today. It works.

EDITOR'S NOTES

This scene-study book has selected 38 speeches from 9 of Moliere's plays, plays that range from his farce to his dark comedy of manners. It must also be reminded that Moliere wrote for actors, and for actors who themselves had a repertoire of schtick which they used and which was expected by the audience to be used. It also needs to be remembered that Moliere wrote comedy, and comedy, to work, usually requires at least two participants—one to set up the joke, and one to react to it. In working with these monologues, it is well for the actor to remember that unless the character is designated as "alone" that there is always someone else on stage reacting to the thoughts of the character, and this reaction added considerably to the humor of the moment. And, lastly, always keep in mind that Moliere is a presentational style of writing and acting. Never exclude the audience from the character's emotions or thoughts or actions.

NOTE ON THE TRANSLATIONS

In the French, SGANARELLE, THE SCHOOL FOR WIVES, TARTUFFE, and THE MISANTHROPE are verse plays. I have chosen deliberately to render all of the selections in this book into English prose for two very personal, and, therefore—I think—two very good reasons. First, French verse plays of the 17th century were written in heroic verse using the Alexandrine line—which is an iambic line of six feet (12 beats to the line). While French lends itself to 12 beats, the natural inclination of the English language is to 10 beats to the line to say it comfortably. (Twelve beats to an English spoken line seems to cause confusion and complicates breath control for some reason.) This is why translators who render Moliere or Racine of Corneille into English verse—be it blank verse or rhymed couplets—recast the writing into iambic pentameter. That's not translating; that's writing the play all over again in a new language and form. Secondly, I am not a poet—nor versifier—and I have no pretensions of having that ability. Therefore, I would not subject my pitiful efforts in such an endeavor to comparison and scrutiny against the masterful and magnificent verse renditions of Moliere's plays by Richard Wilbur, or even the very good ones by Donald M. Frame.

Dick Dotterer

Hollywood, California
January, 1991

—BIOGRAPHICAL NOTE—

Jean-Baptiste Poquelin was born in January, 1622, in Paris, the eldest of six children of a well-to-do upholsterer and furnisher, who later bought the royal title*valet de chambre tapissier ordinaire du Roi.* This attached the family to the Royal retinue, and the elder Poquelin assured that the title is hereditary so that his eldest son would inherit it. To see that he was prepared to serve the king, Jean-Baptiste was schooled at the Jesuit College de Clermont, from which he graduated an excellent student, especially in Latin studies. He then studied for the law, and it is possible that he practiced law for a short time. But in 1643, at the age of 21, he abandoned all of his commercial prospects, changed his name to Moliere, and established with 11 other actors the *Illustre-Theatre.* It was not a success and young Moliere soon found himself in debtors prison, from which his father extracted him. From 1645 to 1658, Moliere and his troupe of actors toured the provinces of France, honing their craft, perfecting their techniques and style, and during this time Moliere became the acknowledged leader of the troupe and began writing plays for them. His first efforts were modelled on the farces of the Italian *commedia dell'arte.* By 1658 Moliere and his actors had gained enough of a reputation and enough provincial patronage to be reintroduced to Paris. Moliere returned to Paris under the patronage of Monsieur—the king's brother; and on October 24, 1658—a date that is memorable in French theatrical history—Moliere and his troupe played before the 20 year old King Louis XIV for the first time. They performed Corneille's tragedy *Nicomede.* It was coolly received, and for the moment the fate of the French theatre hung in the balance. Then Moliere stepped forward and begged the king to allow them to perform as an afterpiece a trifle farce of his own, written in the Italian manner. The king permitted, and the rest, as they say, is history. Moliere and his troupe were allowed to play "officially" in Paris, and Moliere was at once enormously popular, and in time the object of controversy and ecclesiastical malice. He was equally gifted as an actor, director and playwright. In the remaning 15 years of his life, he created classical French comedy with such plays as THE SCHOOL FOR

WIVES, TARTUFFE, THE MISANTHROPE, DON JUAN, THE MISER, and he elevated farce to a true art form with scripts such as THE FORCED MARRIAGE, THE DOCTOR IN SPITE OF HIMSELF, and THE IMAGINARY INVALID. Moliere also enjoyed the friendship and patronage of King Louis XIV. By 1665 Moliere's troupe was under the direct patronage of the king, with a pension of 6,000 francs per year, and allowed to use the title *Troupe du Roi*. The king also stood as godfather to Moliere's infant son. Moliere produced 29 of his existing 33 plays in those last 15 years in Paris, as well as producing fetes and entertainments for the king, and the plays of other writers. For years he had not been in good health, and he worked himself to death. On February 17, 1673, while in the fourth performance of his newest farce, THE IMAGINARY INVALID, Moliere suffered a seizure on stage. He completed the performance, but died an hour later. He was 51 years old.

THE PLAYS OF MOLIERE

THE RIDICULOUS PRECIEUSES
[Les Precieuses ridicules]

There is no real English equivalent to the word "percieuses." The nearest most translators attempt is some deviation of the word "affected." But that is not precisely correct either. The original "precieuses" were a coterie of men and women who met and prided themselves on their literary taste, and called themselves "precieux" and "precieuses." Their first aim was to care for the language and to purify the French from low and vulgar words and expressions that were residue from the earlier civil wars and strife. However, in trying to raise the standards of the language they carried things a bit too far. The "precieuses" and their imitators took things to such an extreme that they seriously injured the language, and in trying to adapt their manners into the refinement they aimed for in their speech, they instigated the most absurd affectations into fashion. They insisted upon the 17th century French equivalent of "buzz" words.

Les Precieuses ridicules was Moliere's first huge success as a writer. It was a one-act play and it took Paris by storm after it's first performance there on November 18, 1659. It was put on as an afterpiece to Corneille's tragedy, *Cinna.* The play is essentially and frankly a farce, but there is a new reality to the characters who, in accord with the tradition of the times, either took stock names (e. g. Mascarille) or the names of the actors playing the roles (e. g. LaGrange or Jodelet). But for Moliere this is the first time as a writer he used his own gifts of observation, dialogue, and mimicry, and did so without, as of yet, abandoning the stock characters of French farce and Italian *commedia dell'arte.*

Magdelon and Cathos are two provincial young ladies who have come to Paris to invade the social world of the capital. They have affected what they think is the dress, speech, and manners of the "precieuses." What they are are two farm girls who believe that a fantasy tour of Hollywood is "for real."

Two suitors, LaGrange and DuCroisy, have been, in their estimation, rudely treated by the young ladies and think the women need a lesson. They send their crude valets to the girls as the Marquis de Mascarille and the Viscomte de Jodelet to woo them. The valets are as affected in their manners as noblemen as the girls are in theirs. The romp of the play is watching this quartet out "precieux" and "precieuses" each other. The joke ends when LaGrange and DuCroisy return to expose the whole charade.

THE RIDICULOUS PRECIEUSES
MAGDELON—SCENE 5

PLAYER: FEMALE   AGE: YOUNG

LaGrange and DuCroisy have been rejected by Magdelon and Cathos as "inelegant" suitors, and they have left the house. Gorgibus, father of Magdelon and uncle of Cathos, has favored the two young men as husbands for the girls, and he is furious with them for scorning the socially established young gentlemen. Both Magdelon and Cathos are, in their turn, highly embarrassed by Gorgibus' "crudeness" and they deplore his dull spirit. They are convinced they cannot be related to such a man. Here, Magdelon explains to her father their view of life and that romance and adventure must happen as it does in the novels of the day.

MAGDELON

O Papa! How extremely bourgeois you are! I am so embarrassed when you talk like that. You ought to learn the fine art of conversation. […] Good heavens! if everyone was just like you, romance would end before it started! It would have been a fine thing if Cyrus the Great had immediately married Mandana, or if Aronce had wedded his Clelia at the beginning of that book. […] My cousin will tell you, Father, just as well as I, that marriage should never occur until after all other adventures have ended. A lover, if he is to be agreeable, should be able to utter fine sentiments, to sigh, to be soft, tender, and passionate. And he must pay court according to the rules. He should first behold she who is to be his future inamorata in church, or on a promenade in a park, or at some public ceremony. Or he should—by fate—

be introduced to her by some friend or relations, preferably at her house. After meeting her, he leaves her presence all pensive and melancholy. The lover must conceal his passion from his beloved for some time, though he makes several visits to her. At these visits, some subject involving gallantry never fails to be brought forth, and this discourse exercises the wit of all present. The day of declaration arrives. This usually should be done while they ambulate in some garden, with everyone else at some distance from them. This declaration is followed by our immediate outrage, which we disclose by blushing and coloring our features, and our fury banishes the lover from our presence for a while. He must find some way to pacify us—which he does, and little by little he accustoms us to hear descriptions of his passion, and he draws from us that confession which causes so much distress. Then comes the adventures: the rivals that thwart established affections, the persecutions by fathers, the jealousies arising from false conclusions from scenes spied upon or conversations reported, the resentments, the despair, the clandestine elopement, and all of its consequences. That is how these matters are conducted in proper, handsome manners; and these are rules that in gentile gallantry cannot be put aside. But to come point blank at the beginning and propose marriage! and to proffer no love before but to offer only a marriage-contract, and to start romance at the back end! Once again, my dear Papa, nothing can be more mechanical than such a proceeding. The mere thought of the idea makes me sick from my head to my toes.

THE RIDICULOUS PRECIEUSES
CATHOS—SCENE 5

PLAYER: FEMALE   AGE: YOUNG

This speech comes right on the heels of Magdelon's just above. Cathos tries to get her uncle to understand what he is apparently refusing to understand by substantiating Magdelon's testimony and reiterating their stance with further evidence.

CATHOS

Uncle, no one could have told you the truth of the matter more exquisitely than my cousin has just done. How can one receive suitors who have only the most grotesque idea of gallantry and whose courtship is so crude? I'll wager they have never seen the Map of Tenderness; and such regions as Fond Epistles, Anxious Minor, Gallant Gestures, and Sweet Verse Village are completely unfamiliar to them. Don't you see how their whole bearing shows it, and they lack that gracious aura that makes a good first impression on other people? They come to court us with not a ribbon attached to their leg; with hats destitute of plumes; with heads lacking coffeured curls; and in coats indigent of adornments! And what is more, I took note that their neckclothes were made by the wrong tailors, and their breeches were not wide enough by more than a good half a foot. Heavens! what kind of lovers are these? What stinginess of apparel! What drab, dreary conversation! It could not be endured! We could not possibly have continued to endure them.

THE RIDICULOUS PRECIEUSES
MAGDELON—SCENE 10

PLAYER: FEMALE   AGE: YOUNG

Magdelon and Cathos have been surprised and honored (and slightly overwhelmed) by the unexpected visitation of the distinguished and socially prominent "Marquis de Mascarille" (LaGrange's valet). He has dazzled the girls with his sophisticated wit, his stylish dress, and his polished social graces. They are convinced that they have at last met the master arbiter of Parisian society. Mascarille has just promised to introduce the girls to prominent literary wits who visit him.

MAGDELON

O! Heavens! We shall be obliged to you, monsieur, obliged to the last degree, if you will do that kindness for us. For, after all, you must be acquainted with all those gentlemen if you would belong to elegant society. They are the ones that make reputations in Paris; and, as you know, a visit from any one of them is enough to establish your acceptance on the inside, even though you have no other qualifications. But what I personally regard, particularly, as most important by these visits is that you learn the hundreds of things that are necessary to know: those things that are the quintessence of sophistication. Everyday you learn gallantry's new witticisms, pretty notes in prose and verse being passed around. You learn as soon as it is done that So-and-So has written the finest piece in the world on some-such subject; or that What's-her-name, the lady, has styled lyrics to this or that tune; or that that person has composed a madrigal upon being granted a woman's favors; and this monsieur has created stanzas on infidelity; Monsieur Zed wrote a six line ode last night to Mademoiselle Tee, who sent him her reply this morning at eight o'clock; Author One has just finished the plot outline to his new book; Author Two is well into the third volume to his new romance; and Author Three has sent his new work to the printers. Knowledge of things such as these is what makes you esteemed in society; and if you are ignorant of them, I would give you not a brass sou for all the wit you might otherwise possess.

SGANARELLE;
or THE IMAGINARY CUCKHOLD
[Sganarelle; ou Le Cocu imaginaire]

SGANARELLE was first acted about six months after the premiere of THE RIDICULOUS PRECIEUSES, on May 28, 1660; and it became Moliere's most frequently produced play during his lifetime. It was his first verse comedy, and it was also the first play in which he performed a character without the traditional mask. Sganarelle is Moliere's invention, and he seems to have a favorite and useful character, for he appears in six other scripts besides this one. Sganarelle is first named in THE FLYING DOCTOR, and then he is prominent in THE SCHOOL FOR HUSBANDS, DON JUAN, THE FORCED MARRIAGE, THE DOCTOR IN SPITE OF HIMSELF, and LOVE'S THE BEST DOCTOR. Whenever Sganarelle appears, he usually represents the weaker, meaner, more selfish, or more cynical side of human nature. He is a clown who strives to rise above his natural elements. (Moliere also always seems to have performed the role whenever the character appeared in a script.)

Contemporary criticism for SGANARELLE ranged from one extreme to another. On one side, Moliere was accused of retreating as an artist by returning to the roots of Italian farce for his sources, and on the other, the play was praised extravagantly for it plotting, its insights, its style, and, most of all, its characters.

The plot of the farce arises from a single incident and a single prop. Celie is engaged and in love with Lelie. Her father, Gorgibus, however, insists she break that engagement and marry a wealthier suitor, Valere. When Celie faints, Sganarelle happens to be passing by. His efforts to revive the girl are seen by his wife, who thinks he's having an affair. Sganarelle jumps to the same conclusion about his wife when he sees her with a locket and overhears her rhapsodizing on the looks of the young man whose miniature portrait is in the locket. (It is Celie's locket. She dropped it when she fainted and Sganarelle's wife found it. The portrait is that of Lelie.) Sganarelle accuses his wife of being unfaithful.

As farce plots would have it, Lelie arrives at this time. He sees that Sganarelle has the locket, asks him where he got it, and the man replies, "From his wife." Lelie assumes that Sganarelle is the old codger that Celie has married, and he faints from shock. The caring business is now reversed, with Sganarelle's wife attempting to revive Lelie. Her actions are observed by both Sganarelle and Celie. Confusion prevails.

SGANARELLE
CELIE'S MAID—SCENE 2

PLAYER: FEMALE   AGE: ANY

The play occurs in a ubiquitous "public square" in Paris, a frequently conventional outdoor setting for popular comedy. Celie has just argued with her father about breaking her engagement with Lelie and obeying his orders to marry Valere. Celie's Maid takes a more pragmatic view of marriage and the need for a husband, rather than support the more romantic idea of a young girl.

CELIE'S MAID

What, madam! Do you so resolutely refuse an offer that so many other women would accept with all their hearts. To frown and grieve when you are offered a husband—and a charming one at that; to delay in this manner, when all you need to utter is a single "Yes!" Well, I wish anyone would marry me! I'm sure I would need no lengthly coaxing; and I certainly wouldn't think it any trouble to say a single "Yes." Believe me, I would prate the word at least a dozen times. Your brother's tutor is a wise man, and one day we were talking about life and other things of the world. He said a woman is like the ivy: it is green and beautiful while it twines around a sturdy tree; but pull it away from the tree and it is limp and is nothing. Dear lady, there is no greater truth than that, as I am a sinner and recipient of woeful experiences. God took my husband, poor Martin, as you know, may Heaven rest his soul. When my husband was alive my complexion was of milk and roses, I was firm and comely, my eyes sparkled with spirit, and my heart was full and content. Even to this moment I lament the loss of my good Martin. In those days of relish, which flashed and were gone like lightning, I never warmed my bed nor slept under an extra blanket, even through the sharpest winters. But now I shiver even in the dogdays of the year. Take my word, madam, there is nothing like having a husband beside you in bed, if only to say "God bless you" if perchance you sneeze.

SGANARELLE
SGANARELLE—SCENE 17

PLAYER: MALE   AGE: ANY

      For his role in this plot, Moliere calls Sganarelle a "bourgeois of Paris." But Sganarelle is not too sure just what his stance should be in this infidelity crisis. As a bourgeois Parisian of the time, he would certainly have been exposed to enough novels and dramas to know that when a husband is cuckhold, it is his duty to be avenged. But he also knows that he has to be very cautious in protecting his own physical safety, especially since he doesn't care much for his name and nothing for his wife. Sganarelle is alone in the public square as he debates with himself just where his "honor" should lead him.

SGANARELLE

[Alone.]
May Heaven protect that dear lady from harm's way! How touching it is that, in her kindness, she wants to avenge me. Her anger, which is provoked by my disgrace, teaches me plainly what I ought to do. No one should suffer quietly such affronts as I bear, unless he is indeed a coward and a fool. I will search out this rascal who abuses and insults me, and I will prove to him that I have the courage to avenge my dishonor. I'll teach you, you cheat, to laugh at my expense and to caress my wife without my leave!

[He strides three or four paces resolutely, then stops.]
Hold! Go gently. This fellow looked as if he could get his blood to boil easily enough; he might, by adding injury upon injury, blister my back as he has decorated my forehead. I dislike from the depths of my soul those fiery tempers who are quick to quarrel, but I have great love for peaceable folk and am warmly disposed toward sensible dispositions. I do not fight, for I fear being beaten; and my greatest trait is my gentle nature. Yet, on the other hand, honor declares that such an affront as this cannot remain unpunished.—Well, let honor say as much as it pleases, and the duce take whoever will listen to it, for all the good it will do me in a pinch. Suppose I now play the hero for once, and as a reward I get three feet of cold, sharp steel thrust through my bread-basket. Tell me, O my honor, when I am dead, and even when the city hears it, will you grow the fatter because of it? The grave is too dismal a cell and too unwholesome a bed for those who are afraid even of the ague. With everything considered, my grave honor, I think, for my part, that I would rather be dishonored and alive than dead with honors thick upon me. What harm's in it, after all? Does it make a man's leg more crooked, or does it spoil his shape? A plague take him who first afflicted the mind with phantom honor, and then linked the honor of the most upright and steady of men with whatsoever fickle woman can do! Since, with good reason, everyone is held responsible for his own misdeeds, why should our honor be held at fault in cases like this? Why should we husbands be blamed for the sins of our wives? If they shamefully misbehave themselves without our permission, we men, it is always true, must bear the blame. They commit the folly, and we are named the fools! It is a vile abuse on one half of a marriage, and the government should remedy such a glaring injustice. Are there not already enough mischances in our lives in spite of all we do? Are there not already quarrels, lawsuits, hunger, thirst, and infirmity to disturb the peace of our lives? Must we stupidly create for ourselves new situations for uneasiness, and torment our souls over things that may have no foundations at all? Let us make a joke and laugh at all of this, despise these foolish fancies, and crush all sighs and tears under our feet. If my wife has done wrong, let her sob buckets; but why should I weep as

well, when I have done nothing? Be everything as it may, I can comfort myself with the knowledge that I am not the only husband so marked. Many worthy men today see their wives courted, and they take no notice. There. No: I will not go and pick a quarrel for what is after all a mere trifle. The world may call me dolt for not avenging myself, but I should look a greater dolt drooping from the point end of a sword.
[He puts his hands on his torso.]
Yet, I feel my bile bubbling again. I feel my anger rising there, and it would push me to some manly action. O! My blood is up! I will be no coward! I will revenge myself on this scoundrel. I will begin at once in this passion that burns within me. I will go throughout the town and tell everyone everywhere that my wife and this thief are deceiving me.
[He Exits.]

∞◊∞◊◊∞◊◊∞◊◊∞◊◊∞◊◊∞◊◊∞◊◊∞◊◊∞◊◊∞◊◊∞◊◊∞◊◊∞◊◊∞◊◊∞◊◊∞◊◊∞◊◊∞

THE SCHOOL FOR WIVES
[L'Ecole de femmes]

In THE SCHOOL FOR WIVES, Sganarelle is replaced by Arnolph. Arnolph is a great advance in Moliere's skill of depicting human nature. In one sweeping characterization the dramatist give us jealously, frustration, and the dupe. But Arnolph also suffers in a genuine way when the Fates conspire to deny him his love and blind him so to his own weaknesses that he cannot admit to have them. Some critics also write that Moliere projected his own fears and his own marital trails into his plays, such as THE SCHOOL FOR WIVES. But before accepting that too readily, temper the decision with the facts that Moliere was first and foremost a man of the theatre, and he knew well that art imitates life. Relationships between the sexes, infidelity (imagined or actual), old men chasing after young girls, young lovers outwitting their watchmen was plot fodder for comedies of the time—and now.

Arnolph is a wealthy bourgeois who has refrained from marriage for twenty years because he is obsessed with the fear of being a cuckhold. He has also gained a not to charitable

10

reputation from his own pitiless derision and stinging attacks on other husbands who have suffered from infidelity. Now he is going to marry rashly, but he thinks he's perfectly safe from the horns. He is going to marry a girl of sixteen, Agnes, whom he has raised for thirteen years, teaching her only what he wants her to know, and inculcating in her only the precepts of marriage with which he agrees. He has trained the "perfect" wife: she is a simpleton. His honor is safe. Safe that is until Agnes happens to meet, quite by accident, the dashing young gallant, Horace. And love suddenly makes her very impetuous.

A SCHOOL FOR WIVES
AGNES—ACT II, SCENE 2

PLAYER: FEMALE   AGE: YOUNG

      Arnolph has assumed the name Monsieur del la Souche, by which he is known in the neighborhood, to his servants, and to Agnes. But he is known as Arnolph to his former friends and to the families of those friends. Arnolph has been away and has just returned home. Outside his house he meets Horace, the son of an old friend, Oronte. Horace, who of course does not know Arnolph's second identity, confides to the older man that he has met and has been courting the most enchanting creature who lives in this house, guarded by an ogre whom he has not met. The creature is, naturally, Agnes; the ogre is—but that would be giving away too much of the plot. Arnolph is furious that his walls have been breached, but before he is convinced that his honor has already been sullied, he will interrogate Agnes. He knows that she is so innocent and trusting of him that she will tell him that truth without guile. Arnolph and Agnes are strolling about the square as he casually asks her of her activities in his absence and of the rumors that while he was gone a young man was seen being entertained by her. Arnolph knows, he says, this isn't true. Agnes, in her utter trust and innocence, tells him it is true, and then tells him how and why it happened.

AGNES

[To ARNOLPH.]
I was sitting on my balcony, working in the fresh air, when I saw a handsome man—a very fine young man— passing along under those trees right over there. When he saw he had caught my eye, he immediately bowed to me in a most respectful way. And I, not to be thought impolite, returned his bow with a curtsey of my own. He bowed again, suddenly, and what else could I do, but immediately make another curtsey of my own. He bowed to me a third time, and I, of course, instantly answered his bow with a third curtsey of my own. He passed back and forth all that afternoon, and each time he passed me, he made to me the lowest and most solemn of bows. And each time he bowed—I never took my eyes off of him—I made a curtsey to him. If night had not come on, I would have continued returning a curtsey for each of his bows, for I was unwilling to yield first, or to be thought by him to be less polite than he. [...] The next day, as I stood at our door, and old woman approached me and said to me: "My child, may God from his Heaven bless you and long let you keep your beauty. God has not made you such a lovely creature for you to use His gifts badly. You should know that you have wounded a heart so greatly that now, in such pain, it is forced to cry aloud and complain!" [...]
—Me! I have wounded someone? I exclaimed, quite astonished.
—Yes, wounded! she cried. You have wounded him severely. It is the young man you saw from your balcony yesterday.
—Alas, I answered, how could I possibly wound him? Did I drop something on him carelessly and am unawares of it?
—No, she replied. It is your eyes—your eyes that did the deed. It is from your glance that he has received the fatal stroke that cause his hurt.
—Good faith! I said. I am astonished beyond words. Do my eyes have a fatal power that can do others harm?
—Oh, yes, my daughter, she cried. Your eyes are filled with a deadly poison which is unknown to you. To come to the point, the poor boy languishes, and if—this charitable old lady told me then—if you are so cruel as not to help him, he will be dead and buried within two days' time.

—Heaven preserve me, I cried. I should be very sorry for it! But what help can I give him?

—My child, she cried, he only wants the happiness of seeing you and talking to you. Your eyes alone can save him from death, only they are the medicine to remedy the mischief they have done.

—Is that all? I said. Then will all my heart, and if that be all, tell him he may come see me as often as he likes! [...] That's how he came to see me, and was cured. Don't you yourself now think I had reason to do as I did? Could I, after all, have it weighing on my conscience to let him die when I could help him? I who am so full of compassion for everything that suffers, that I can't see a chicken killed without crying. [...] Why, what's the matter, monsieur? You seem to be displeased. Did I do something amiss in what I have told you?

THE SCHOOL FOR WIVES
ARNOLPH—ACT III, SCENE 2

PLAYER: MALE   AGE: MATURE

Arnolph feels that he has dealt with the Horace problem by ordering Agnes to deny him entrance to the house, and to reject him rudely—from the safe distance of her chamber window. He also now feels it's time to inform the girl of the reason for his return: that he intends to make her his wife, and in doing so, there are certain obligations he expects from her in marriage.

ARNOLPHE

[To AGNES.]
Put your work away, Agnes, and listen to me. Lift your head up a little, and turn your face toward me.
(He points his finger at his forehead)
There;—look at me right there while I talk to you. Listen to me carefully, and remember every word I say to you. Agnes, I am

going to marry you; and a hundred times a day you ought to think how blessed you are to be in this situation, considering the humble condition you were in, when, in my benevolent goodness, I raised you from the station of a lowly peasant girl to that by marriage to the honorable bourgeois; to enjoy both the bed and caresses of a man who has always shunned the bonds of marriage. You should never forget how insignificant you would be without this union to me; you should daily consider upon this, so that you always deserve the station to which I raise you, and to make you know your place so that I never have to regret what I do for you with this alliance. Marriage, Agnes, is no trifle; there are severe duties required of the wife; and I have no intention to give you ascension to that position to let you live a free and pleasurable life. The female is dependent in a marriage, and all power is invested in the husband. Marriage is thought to be the merging of two parts into one body; but those two parts are by no means equal; one part is supreme, while the other part is abject; one half governs, the other half submits; the obedience the disciplined soldier shows to his commander, the servant to his master, the child to his father, even the lowliest monk to his abbot does not even approach the malleability, the humility, the submission, the profound deference which the wife should manifest for her husband, who is her chief, master, and lord. When he looks at her seriously, the wife should lower her eyes groundward immediately, and not look again at his face until he deigns to give her a gracious glance. Wives today little understand this, but you are not to follow the examples of other women. Do not imitate those vile jades, whose escapades are the talk of the whole city. And don't let the Devil tempt you: that is to say, do not listen to the mooings of every young swain. You must consider, Agnes, that when I make you part of me, I entrust my honor to you; and this honor is tender: it is easily hurt. This is no trifling subject just for afternoon conversation. In Hell there are boiling cauldrons in which wives who have lived wicked lives are plunged for ever and ever. These are not idle stories I tell you, and these lessons should be ensconced in your heart. If you adhere to them sincerely, avoid being a coquette, your soul will remain pure and white as the lily. But if you stain your honor, your soul will become black as coal;

everyone will see you as a hideous creature, and one day you will be dragged into Hell as the Devil's property, there to boil in those cauldrons for all eternity. But may Heaven's mercy keep you from that fate. Now, make curtsey to me. As a novice in a convent must know by heart the rules of her order, so should a new bride know the rules of her office. I have in my pocket a book of great importance. It will instruct you in your duties as a wife. I don't know the author, but his work measures him a worthy soul. I would have this book be your only study. [...] By and by, I'll explain all matters to you as they should be explained, line by line. [...] Go in, and take special care of that valuable book.

THE SCHOOL FOR WIVES
ARNOLPH—ACT III, SCENE 3

PLAYER: MALE   AGE: MATURE

Arnolph is very pleased with his activities and with himself so far in his handling of Horace, and breaking the marriage news to Agnes. He has just listened to her read several of the "Maxims on Marriage, the Duties of a Wife, and her Daily Exercises," from the book he has just given her. Agnes has just left Arnolph, and, O, he is pleased with himself and his present circumstances. He's proving to himself that he has been correct in his methods all along.

ARNOLPH

[Alone.]
I can find no better girl to make my wife than her. I shall be able to mold her life just as I am pleased to do. She is like a piece of wax between my hands, and I can shape her however I please. In my absence, it is true, I was nearly a victim through her excessive innocence. But to tell the truth, it is better for a wife to stumble—if she should stumble at all—from that cause, for such mistakes can be easily rectified. A simple person is ready to be

taught, and if she should stray from the straight and narrow path, then a word or two in reprimand will bring her immediately onto the path again. But a cunning wife is another kind of creature altogether. Her husband's fate hinges only upon her whim. Nothing can divert her from the course she chooses, once she sets upon it. And all our teachings prove only so many words. She uses her wit to make a mockery of our principles, she makes her faults her virtues, and she devises ways to trick even the cleverest man in order to accomplish her wicked wiles. There is no way to stem her flow; an intelligent woman is a she-devil at intrigue, and if she decides to pass a silent verdict on her husband's honor, there is nothing left to be done but submit to it. Believe me, a great many honest men will admit to that. But that foolish swain—my young "rival"—shall find no cause to strut and beam. He has tattled too much and he will meet with that he deserves. This is a common fault among Frenchmen: when they are lucky in a love affair, they cannot bear to keep it a secret. They are so vain that they would rather hang than not tell about it. Surely a woman must be baited by the Devil to trust such brainless boobs with flapping tongues! And—But here he comes! I will be upon my guard, and find out just how defeated he is.

THE SCHOOL FOR WIVES
ARNOLPH—ACT III, SCENE 5

PLAYER: MALE   AGE: MATURE

But all is not well on the home front. Horace just imparted the news to Arnolph that he (Horace) has been barred from the house, and that Agnes has pelted him with stones. Ah! But all is not lost to young love. One of the stones had a love letter wrapped around it. Horace, in his fervor to share every-thing with his friend, reads the letter to Arnolph, much to the older man's chagrin. Agnes has found a means to thwart Arnolph's carefully laid plans. Horace has just left Arnolph, after asking the other man if he could help him find a way to gain entrance to Monsieur de la Souche's house.

ARNOLPH

[Alone.]
What mortification I suffered at the hands of that young rapscallion. How I had to struggle to conceal the torment of my pain! How can a simple girl have the wit to conceive such ready tricks? Either she has pretended her innocence all this time, or else the Devil has breathed treachery into her soul. I thought that cursed letter would kill me! That rascal has taken possession of her mind; he has dislodged me and firmly planted himself there. This drives me to despair, and gives me mortal pain. My suffering is doubled by the theft of her love, for not only do I lose her heart, I lose my honor as well. It infuriates me to find my place usurped, and it maddens me to see that my prudent schemes have gone all for naught. I know that to punish her guilty passion, I need only to leave her to her evil ways, and I will be avenged on her by her own wicked deserts. But still, it is very woeful to lose the one you love. Gracious Heavens! I used my philosophy to choose her. Why then am I bewitched by her? She has no family, no friends, no fortune; she betrays my care, my benevolence, my love. And yet I love her, even after this base deception, so much so that I cannot give her up. O, Fool! Have you no shame?! I rage! I rave! I'm a disgrace. I could box mine own ears a thousand times! I'll go inside for a little while, but only to see what face she shows after such perfidy. Please Heaven that my brow not sprout a pair of horns. But if it be so decreed, that I must suffer this, grant me the strength others have shown, that in my shame I may show the firmness I see in others about me.

THE SCHOOL FOR WIVES
ARNOLPH—ACT IV, SCENE I

PLAYER: MALE   AGE: MATURE

Arnolph is beginning to feel the pressures of his world spiralling out of control, and he works feverishly to keep control of his plans, and prevail over Horace and adversarial circumstances. This speech opens Act IV, and comes immediately on the heels of the speech just previous.

ARNOLPH

[Alone.]
I am so restless I cannot stay put in any one place for long. My mind is plagued with a thousand cares, how to manage things both inside the house and out, how to put a stop to the feckless intents of this young coxcomb. With what equanimity the wretched girl greeted me. She is not at all concerned at what she has done, though she has borne me to within an inch of my grave. One would swear, to see her, that she is the portrait of peaceful purity. The more I watched her, the more I was enraged; the more I boiled, the more my heart upsurged and inflamed with passionate ardor for her. I was embittered, vexed, desperate; yet I had never seen her look so beautiful. Her eyes had never been so incandescent, never before had they roused in me such inordinate desire. My soul knows that it will kill me if I do not make Agnes my bride. What? Have I raised her with such tenderness and with so many precautions—I have had her in my house since her infancy—have I built my fondest hopes on her, have I, with fondness, watched her grow toward womanhood, have I for thirteen years trained her character to my specifications so that some silly boy, with whom she is in love, can come and carry her off under my very nose—especially when she is almost already married to me? No, by Heavens, no! No, my brash young friend, no! By Heaven's breath, no! Try as hard as you like, my young fool, but I shall not allow your plots to overthrow my plans. By my faith, I shall abort your

misguided hopes. And you will find you'll have no cause to laugh at me!

THE SCHOOL FOR WIVES
HORACE—ACT IV, SCENE 6

PLAYER: MALE   AGE: YOUNG

Horace is dazzling, handsome, young, dashing, and thoroughly infatuated (or in love) with Agnes. But he is not one of the great creative intellects of his age. If he saw a basket with two apples and two oranges in it, he would never refer to it as a basket with four pieces of fruit. To him, they would always remain two apples and two oranges. It has never occured to Horace that every time he confides something to Monsieur Arnolph that his next encounter with Agnes is encumbered by Monsieur de la Souche. It has never dawned on Horace that the only time he can find Arnolph is in this neighborhood, a neighborhood far removed from where the house of Monsieur Arnolph is located. And Monsieur Arnolph never seems to have pressing business in the neighborhood. Horace considers his encounters with Monsieur Arnolph nothing more than happy coincidences. And here the young man happens to chance upon another such meeting, perhaps the most important meeting of them all.

HORACE

[Entering; to ARNOLPH.]
I'm always in luck to find you in this neighborhood. I just had a narrow escape, I can tell you. Just now, as I left you, I happened by chance to catch sight of Agnes on her balcony, enjoying the cool breeze from the trees near-by. She signaled me, then she came downstairs to the garden, and she opened the gate for me. We both went upstairs to her chamber, but we were barely in her room when she heard her jealous guardian ascend the stairs. All she could do in such a dangerous pinch was to

19

shut me in her wardrobe, amongst her dresses. None too soon, either, for he came directly into her room. I didn't see him, but I heard him. He strode across the room, to and fro, without speaking a word, but he emitted pitiful sighs now and again, which illustrated his woes. Sometimes he hammered the table with his fist, striking a little dog that fawned about him; whatever he found in his way that he could throw about, he flung in his mad manner about the room. At one time, in his raging passion, he knocked every flower vase from off the mantelpiece, where my lady had placed them. From this display, I have no doubt the old goat has learned of the trick she played on him and fears still another set of horns. After some time, having vented his anger on all hapless objects he could seize, that invidious, agitated gentleman left her room without even saying what disturbed him—and I came out of hiding. We couldn't venture to stay together longer, it was much too dangerous. But tonight, when it's late, I'll gain entrance to her chamber. I shall cough three times outside her window. That shall be the signal. Agnes will open her window and with the assistance of a ladder and Agnes' aid, love will try to mount the obstacles and place me at my love's side. I tell you this because you are my sole friend. Joy increases by being revealed. One could taste the utmost bliss a hundred times over, yet it would be flat and unsatisfactory if no one else knows about it. You, as well, I believe, will be pleased at the success of my affairs. Adieu: I have many urgent preparations to make.

THE SCHOOL FOR WIVES
ARNOLPH—ACT IV, SCENE 7

PLAYER: MALE   AGE: MATURE

Horace has just left Arnolph alone with his thoughts after informing him of the plot to elope with Agnes that night. This speech comes directly on the heels of Horace's exit at the end of the previous speech. It is one of the two speeches in the play that points toward the climax of Arnolph's actions and frustrations.

ARNOLPH

[Alone.]

O! Will my persecuting stars never allow me time for a fresh breath of air? Blow follows blow! Am I fated to see all my prudence and vigilance defeated by them? And shall I, at my age in life, be made a fool by a simpleton of a girl and this rantipoling youth? For twenty years, like a discerning philosopher, I watched the unhappy destiny of husbands of this age, and I have carefully catalogued all those accidents which have brought even the most sagacious of them low and have thought to profit from knowing those things that brought them to disgrace. When I decided to take a wife, I sought to save my forehead from a pair of horns, to protect it from reaching the same level as theirs. Toward this noble end, I thought I had taken all the precautions human knowledge could devise. But, as if it were decreed by Fate that no man on earth could be exempt from it, after all the insight and experience I have gathered on these affairs, after twenty years of thought on how to conduct a marriage project with prudence and caution, have I avoided the common paths so many husbands have followed only to find myself, after all, at the same place as they? No! foul destiny, no! I'll still make liar of you! I still have in my power the desired object. And if her heart has been stolen from me by this hateful coxcomb, I will at least prevent him from stealing anything else. Tonight, chosen for their elopement, will not pass as agreeably as they intend. It affords me some pleasure, in the midst of all my misfortune, to be well informed of all the plots and snares they set against me; and to think that this thoughtless blunderer, who thinks of outwitting me, makes a confidant of his own arch rival.

THE IMPROMPTU AT VERSAILLES
[L' Impromptu de Versailles]
MOLIERE—SCENE 3

PLAYER: MALE   AGE: ANY

THE IMPROMPTU AT VERSAILLES seems to have been planned, written, and performed all within one week. Rumor has it that King Louis XIV encouraged Moliere to revenge himself on his enemies, and put the Court theatre at his disposal for that expressed purpose. The little play was first produced on October 14, 1663. Moliere chose the scheme of a "play-within-a-play." This permitted him to discuss the nature of theatre and actors, to explore the principles of theatre, and to attack his enemies through the means of "professional" differences. Polemically, the intent of the play is clear, but by the use of Moliere on stage as Moliere, the play is important because his intense expressions on stage theory and practice may be the most believable utterances on such things by him that we possess. Moliere was a complete man of the theatre. He also knew where his energies must be focused and whom he must please if he were to remain successful and in favor.

MOLIERE

You anger me when you talk like that. You women seem particularly obsessed with this madness. You would have me ignite into flames, and, following their example, rage against them straightaway with invectives and abuses. Much honor would there be for me in that. And such aggravation would I give them! Are they not just waiting for that sort of thing? When they were deliberating whether to perform that play of theirs—*Portrait of a Painter*—do you think they did not wonder about a counter-attack? And what do you suppose some of them answered: "Let him insult us all he wants after the production, as long as we make our money." A mind like that is not sensible to shame. And wouldn't I get a fine revenge if I gave them exactly what they wanted? [...] The only harm I have done them is this: I have had the good fortune to be more successful than they

22

wished me to be; our audiences laugh more loudly than theirs do. Everything they've done since we arrived is Paris shows only too well what they envy about us. Let them do what they please; all of their undertakings will not disturb me. If they criticize my plays, so much the better. Heaven forfend I should ever write a play that would please them. Now that would be a bad business for me. [...] But what do I care if they charp and grumble? Have I not received from my comedy all I could wish to receive from it, since it pleases the august persons at Court whom I particularly strive to please? Don't I have reason to be pleased by its success? And don't their cheap cracks come too late? I ask you: am I now the one who is chiefly concerned? When they attack a piece that is successful are they not attacking the King and his court, who applaud it? [...] And you are also foolish. What a fine topic for a court entertainment—Monseiur Boursault! I would like to know how anyone could make him amusing. He would be happy enough to be the subject of a burlesque on a stage. It would be the only way he could get a laugh. It would be too great an honor for him to be ridiculed before such a distinguished audience. There could be no more he could wish. He attacks me with gaiety in his heart, his sole purpose is to make himself known, no matter how it is done. He is a man with nothing to lose. The players at the Bourgogne have set him against me with no other purpose than to engage me in a silly quarrel; they hope to sap my energy with this quarrel so I will have no time for other plays I have to write. And you are mad enough to fall into their snare! But I will make a public declaration: I do not intend to make any answer to their criticisms or countercriticisms. Let them say the worst things they can about my plays; I agree to it. Let them try to pick up the bones of my plays after we've finished with them, let them turn them inside out, like a jacket, for their theatre, and let them endeavor to profit from whatever good things they may find in them and from my good fortune; I consent to it. They need the help of better material, and I am very glad to contribute to their support—provided they are content with what I can decently grant them. Courtesy does have its limits; there are some things that neither the audience nor he who is being satirized find funny. I willing give up to them my plays, my face, my gestures, my words, my tone of voice, my mannerisms. They may do and say what they please with them—if they can make good use of them. I don't oppose their use of these things, and shall be overjoyed if such things can raise a laugh. But when I give them all of these, they ought to do me the favor of leaving the rest to me. They should not touch those subjects, as I hear they do, which they accuse me of in their plays. This is what I must civilly request of the honorable gentleman whom they have hired to write their pieces. And that is the only answer they shall have from me. [...] Let's say no more about it. We're wasting time in chatter and speeches rather than rehearsing the play. Now: where were we? I've forgotten.

∞∞

TARTUFFE;
OR THE IMPOSTER
[Tartuffe; ou L' Imposteur]

It took Moliere five years to gain permission for a public performance of TARTUFFE. It was finished in a three-act form in 1664 and played before the king. It aroused such controversy that even with the king's support Moliere could not be safely granted a license for public performance until 1669. TARTUFFE was first seen by the general public on February 5, 1669. It was such an enormous success that is played for 48 nights, a most unusual number of performances for that time. It is the one play that is said never to have been out of the repertoire of the *Comedie-Francaise* from its founding in 1680 to this date. It is also one of the three plays, along with THE MISANTHROPE and DON JUAN, that may be short-listed as Moliere's masterpiece. Moliere created the part of Orgon.

The controversy surrounding TARTUFFE is centered around the mistaken criticism that the play is about religious hypocrisy (and we all know that *all* priests and preachers are ordained by God and thus are pure and would never use religion, the Church, nor the faith of others for their own advancement and gains). TARTUFFE is about gullibility. Tartuffe is not a religious hypocrite because he is not religious. He is a con man

24

who uses religion as a vehicle for his scam. Orgon is a mark—
and God save the mark!

Orgon believes that all men possess the same integrity
and righteousness that he does. He sees all men as clones of his
own character. And he accepts men only on the evidence they
present to him. So, it is not surprising that Orgon would be
duped by Tartuffe and that he would take the man into his
household on open faith. But Tartuffe fools no one in his house
but Orgon. However, Orgon is so obsessed with Tartuffe and
his "goodness" that he rejects all other opinions of the man. The
only one to agree with Orgon is his mother, Madam Pernelle.
Tartuffe, for his part, uses his influence over Orgon to take
control of the man, his life, and his household. Tartuffe manages to have Orgon alienate and disinherit his children; ma-
nipulates Orgon to allow him opportunities to seduce the man's
wife; gain control of all his wealth; and gain access to his secrets
and private papers. All of which, he plans to use at the proper
time to rout Orgon and become master of the house rather than a
guest.

TARTUFFE
MADAM PERNELLE—ACT I, SCENE 1

PLAYER: FEMALE   AGE: MATURE

The play opens with Orgon's mother, Madam Pernelle,
leaving his house in a rage from her disagreement with everyone
else over the character and conduct of that worthy and pious
man, Tartuffe. Madam Pernelle is in no mood to listen to argu-
ments any more, and she is at odds with her daughter-in-law,
Elmire; Elmire's brother, Cleante; her two grandchildren,
Marianne and Damis; and even Marianne's maid, the brash
Dorine.

MADAM PERNELLE

[To ELMIRE.]
These, daughter, are the fairy tales told to please your ears. No one else may get a word in edgewise in this house as long as Madam Maid, here, chatters on and on all day. But I shall be heard, and I mean to have my say. I tell you the wisest thing my son has ever done is to take this holy man into his family. Heaven, in its mercy, sent Tartuffe here just when he was needed most, to save your souls, to make all of you repent. For your salvation, listen to Tartuffe. Whatever he reproves deserves reproof. These visitors, these dances, this idle chatter you enjoy are all inventions of the Devil. You never hear conversations on pious matters, only tittle-tattle and gossip on nonsensical things. Often, too, our neighbors become the brunts for their share, and slander is spoken everywhere. In short, a sensible person loses his senses and his head spins at such gatherings, just from the confusion and sounds. A thousand idle stories all start at the same time, everyone must have his say at once. It was astutely pointed out the other day by a friend of mine, a doctor of theology, that this is a perfect Tower of Babel—for everyone babbles on until he can babble no more. And to illustrate his point, he said....
[Points at CLEANTE.]
There, you see: your brother is snickering already. Well, sir, what's the joke? Go and find your foolish friends and there laugh your fill. Don't...
[To ELMIRE.]
I could say more, but I've said all I will. Farewell to you, daughter. Know that I don't have half the esteem for this house that I once did. It will be long days before I set foot inside yours doors again.
[Exit.]

TARTUFFE
DORINE—ACT I, SCENE 2

PLAYER: FEMALE   AGE: ANY

Madam Pernelle has left Orgon's house in full sail, with the family members trailing in her wake. Dorine, the brash and very vocal maid to Orgon's daughter, Marianne, is left to talk to Elmire's brother, Cleante. Dorine possesses the common sense to see what is there, and she was born with the democratic notion that everyone is equal and should be talked to on equal basis, especially when one is making a fool of himself. Dorine knows her place as a maid in the household, but she also knows that one of her duties is to protect the members of the household, even from their own actions, and to do that she has an obligation to speak plainly. And though she shows deference to Cleante, she has no fear to speak her mind bluntly to him because she knows he will listen and that he too is sensible and a worried man about his sister's family.

DORINE

[To CLEANTE.]
Oh, truly, Madam Pernelle is besotted with Tartuffe, but all that is nothing compared to the infatuation of her son. Were you to see him, you would be astonished at how he is so much more the worse. During our civil wars, Orgon gained the reputation of a man of good sense, and he showed courage while in the service of his king. But since he's become enchanted with Tartuffe, he's become almost silly. He calls Tartuffe "brother," and loves him with a heart a hundred times greater than he gives to his mother, son, daughter, or his wife. He makes Tartuffe his sole confidant and confides only to him all his secrets, and has made him the prudent overseer of his behavior. He pampers him, pets him, caresses him—I tell you a mistress could not expect better attention. He places Tartuffe in the place of honor at table, and he delights in watching him gulp down enough food to feed six people. The very best cuts and tenderest vegetables are for him, and if he belches, our master bids him a

"God Bless You." In short, Orgon dotes on him; Tartuffe is everything to him—his hero. He admires all his actions, quotes him at every opportunity, sees every trivial thing Tartuffe does as a wonder, and every word he says is as if an oracle just recited. Tartuffe understands this man, and he means to make his profit by him. He knows how to impose on Orgon a hundred different ways. By his sanctimonious cant he swindles money from him, and on the strength of his hypocritical bigotry, he takes it upon himself to reprove the whole household and family. Even that hooligan boy who acts as Tartuffe's servant dares to chide us all. He comes in and preaches to us with fierce, indignant looks, and he throws away our ribbons, our rouges, and our patches. The other day, this wretched hoodlum tore a fine handkerchief to pieces because he found it folded between two pages of that pious work, *Flower of the Saints.* He said we committed an abominable sin by pairing a holy book with the adornments of Hell.

TARTUFFE
ORGON—ACT I, SCENE 6

PLAYER: MALE   AGE: MATURE

Orgon has returned home from an absence to be greeted by the maid Dorine and his brother-in-law, Cleante. Before he does anything else, he says he must inquire as to the status of his house and how it faired during his absence. To all reports about anyone but Tartuffe, he seems indifferent at best. But as to his inquiries as to the well-being of Tartuffe, no matter what the answer (the answer is always positive), Orgon replies "The poor man!" After Dorine leaves Orgon, Cleante remarks that she is making fun of her master, and he for one doesn't blame her. He then begins to try to discuss Orgon's obsession with Tartuffe. To this, Orgon gives him short shrift.

ORGON

[To CLEANTE.]

Not another word, Cleante. You do not know the man of whom you speak. [...] Brother, you would delight with him if you but knew him. And you would never get over your wonder. He is a man who...ah! a man...in short, a man! Whoever carefully follows his teachings lives in a most profound peace of mind, and the rest of the world becomes a dunghill to him. Oh, yes, I'm quite another man since befriended by him. He teaches me to free myself from all affection, he detaches my soul from all ties of earthly love and friendship. I should see my brother, children, mother, and wife die and I would not care about it. [...] If only you had seen him when I first met him, you would feel for him the same love that I do. He came to church everyday, and with the mildest behavior knelt down right before me on both his knees. He attracted the attention of the whole congregation by the fervent way he sent his prayers to Heaven, wrapped in saintly ecstasy. He sighed deeply, and time and again, he humbly kissed the ground. When I would leave, he would move quickly before me, and offer me holy water at the door. His servant boy, who is as devout as he, told me his name and of his poverty. I made him small gifts, but with the utmost modesty he always returned part of it back to me. "This is too much," he would say. "Too much by half. I am unworthy of your pity." And when I refused to take back any of what I had given him, he distributed it to the poor, right where I could watch him do it. At last, Heaven inspired me to take him into my house, and since he has been here, everything has flourished. He censors everything, of course; and with regard to my wife, he takes extreme care of my honor. He warns me of potential admirers who cast amorous eyes upon her, and he is a dozen times more jealous of her than I have ever been. And you've no idea of the extent of the man's pious fervors. He accuses himself of sin with every trifle; the most insignificant thing is enough to shock him. Why, there other day, he berated himself for having caught a flea while at his prayers, and then having killed it with a pinch too fierce.

TARTUFFE
TARTUFFE—ACT III, SCENE 3

PLAYER: MALE   AGE: ANY

In his quest to gain control of the Orgon's household, Tartuffe has asked for the hand of the daughter, Marianne, who is already engaged to Valere. Tartuffe's object is Marianne's inheritance. However, Tartuffe is physically attracted to Elmire, Orgon's beautiful second wife. There are two scenes in the play in which Tartuffe is exposed trying to seduce Elmire. This is the first one.

TARTUFFE

[To ELMIRE.]
My heart, madam, as you must know is not made of stone.[…] To love beauty which is of the eternal does not stifle in us a love which is more fleeting and of the earth; and we can easily be charmed by Heaven's perfect creations. It's glories shine forth in creatures such as you; but in you alone are Heaven's choicest wonders centered. It has lavished on you its rarest wonders and dearest charms which dazzle the eye and touch the heart. I have never gazed upon you, perfect creature, without admiration for the Creator and the Universe, and without feeling my heart seized with the most ardent love for the most beautiful self-portrait God has painted. At first, I feared that this secret passion was some snare the Devil had laid. I even resolved to avoid your company for fear that you would prove an obstacle to my salvation. But I have recognized, O gracious beauty, that my passion need not be a guilty one. I could reconcile it with propriety, and I have given my whole soul over to it. I am presumptuous, I know, to offer a heart as poor as mine to you like this, but in my love I hope everything from you, and nothing from the efforts of my worthless self. You are my hope, my happiness, my peace. Only you can decide if I will be forever happy or abjectly miserable. […] Although I am pious, I am no less a man. When one sees your celestial beauties, the heart surrenders and reasons no more. I know that coming from

me, madam, such a confession seems somewhat strange; but, after all, I am no angel, and if you condemn this confession I make, you have only your own attractiveness to blame. As soon as I first saw your superhuman beauty, my whole being surrendered to you. Your divine charms became the sovereign of my heart; your tenderness overcame everything—my fasting, my prayers, my tears. I fixed all my hopes in you. My eyes and sighs have told you this a thousand times. Today, I tell it to you in words. Oh, if you would consider the tribulations and trials of this, your unworthy slave, with some kindness, if you would be compassionate towards me, if you would deign to stoop so low as to my nothingness, you would have from me, O marvellous creature, a devotion never to be equalled. Your reputation would be safe in my hands: there would be no disgrace, no notoriety. The fops at court upon whom the ladies dote are far too noisy and have a tendency to boast. They are ever vain in their successes, and each new favor is quickly revealed. Their indiscreet tongues abuse the trust of the objects of their adoration. But men like me burn with a hidden fire. We know how to love discreetly, and to keep it permanently secret. The care we take to preserve our own good name is the guarantee to the woman who accepts our heart. She will find love without scandal, pleasure without fear.

TARTUFFE
ELMIRE—ACT IV, SCENE 5

PLAYER: FEMALE   AGE: YOUNG

This is the second scene in the play in which Tartuffe attempts to seduce Elmire. Orgon completely disbelieved the evidence of the first seduction attempt, even though his own son, Damis, was hidden in a cabinet and interrupted the attempt before Elmire could defend herself no more. The result of that scene was for Orgon to disown Damis, to exile him from the house, and to turn the chaperoning of his wife over the Tartuffe. Elmire decides that desperate measures are now called for. She decides that in order to get Orgon to believe them, she is going to have to put her honor on the line for the second time. Only this time, to guarantee that Orgon is an eye-witness to Tartuffe's actions and designs, Elmire insists that Orgon be in the room, sequestered under a table (hidden by a large drape over it). Because of the ruckus created by the last seduction attempt, Tartuffe is more cautious about Elmire's intentions, and he must first be won over. This is the beginning of the famous "table scene" of the play.

ELMIRE

[To TARTUFFE.]
I have an important secret to reveal to you, Tartuffe. But first, shut the doors before I speak, and make sure no one is near so as to overhear us.
(TARTUFFE goes to shut the doors and returns.]
It will never do to have a mishap as the one this morning occur again. Never was I so taken by surprise in my life, and Damis put me in a terrible panic because of you. You saw how I tried to baffle his purpose and to calm his anger. I was so greatly confused that I never thought of denying his accusations. But, thank Heaven, the results are all for the better, and because of it, things are on much safer ground. Your reputation quelled the storm; my husband cannot be suspicious of you. And to show his defiance for the slanderous rumors, he wishes us to be constantly together. Therefore, I can be locked in this room with you alone and have no fear of engendering gossip. I also feel that I am now allowed to open my heart to you—but perhaps I am to forward in answering your suit. [...] Oh, if my earlier refusal has offended you, then how little you know of a woman's heart or what we try to convey when we resist with such a feeble defense. At such times our modesty always struggles against any emotion the lover inspires. However we may justify submitting to love, there is always a certain shame attached to the admission of it. At first we fight against it, but it should be easy to see from our manner that our hearts have been surrendered. It is simply for the sake of honor that our lips refuse to give words to our desires. And with our refusals, we

promise everything. I feel I am too open with you in my confession, but since I have begun, I will finish. Tell me, would I have struggled to restrain Damis, do you think, would I have listened to your declaration, so composed and mute, if your offer had not been a pleasure to me? When I tried on my own part to get you to refuse the marriage to Marianne just announced, did not my urgency suggest to you that I was overwhelmingly interested in you, and that I would suffer great anguish if by such a marriage you would make me share a heart and affection that I wanted wholly for mine own!

∞∞

DON JUAN;
OR THE FEAST OF THE STATUE
[Don Juan; ou Le Festin de pierre]

DON JUAN, which was first performed on February 15, 1665, is a play about hypocrisy. It was written shortly after the first production of TARTUFFE in its three-act form and the controversy that version engendered. It is easy to tell that TARTUFFE and its reception was very much on Moliere's mind as he wrote DON JUAN. DON JUAN seems to have been written as a counterpart to TARTUFFE, and this script is more bold and more philosophic than its celebrated sister play. This play has never been banned because in it Moliere attacks an abstract idea rather than a class of people, as he did in TARTUFFE. It was the class, not the idea, that prevented the performances of TARTUFFE. And in the fifth act of DON JUAN, Moliere reeks his revenge on that class.

Moliere needed a new play, since TARTUFFE was forbidden, to keep his theatre open. The subject of Don Juan was in the air and on the stages at the time. Don Juan makes his first noted appearance in dramatic literature in the Spanish play THE TRICKSTER OF SEVILLE by Tirso de Molina. To Molina and the writers that followed Don Juan presented little problem—he was the wicked seducer who is finally punished by God. Then Moliere took up the Don (about a hundred years before Mozart and da Ponte put their touch on him) and the whole story took on a different hue. Into this seducer's story and world, Moliere

33

created some things that were completely new. First is the complexity of the relationship between Don Juan and his bumbling valet, that old friend of the audience, Sganarelle. And there are the good qualities Moliere gave to Don Juan: his courage and pride, his curious honesty, his complex generosity. Yet, in even a more forthright way than in TARTUFFE, Moliere expounds on his theme that the ordinary man of right-mindedness is often weak and infused with superstition; that a wicked hypocrite is a terrible curse to the people he encounters; and that no human can check a clever hypocrite. In the case of Don Juan it takes a miracle and his destruction by that miracle to make the world safe from him.

The story of Don Juan is, in itself, a familiar one. Juan has married Donna Elvire (one of many women he has married without annulment or divorce in between) and has deserted her. She has followed him to Sicily, where this play is set. Juan spurns Donna Elvire and says he should return her to the convent whence he stole her. Don Juan pursues his pleasures and in that pursuit he is shipwrecked, and rewards his rescuer by trying to seduce his girl friend. Don Juan is trailed by Donna Elvire's brothers, and Juan saves one of them from highwaymen, and shows a great deal of bravery doing it. He refuses to identify himself, but tells the brother that Don Juan will meet him "on a field of honor." Finally, the Don's journeys take him to the tomb of a commander whom he killed. He mocks the tomb and the statue of the commander, and invites the statue to dinner. The statue nods his acceptance of the invitation.

By Act IV, Moliere stresses the Don's defiance of the supernatural (i. e., God). Donna Elvire pleads with him to change, or Heaven plans for him a bad end. The Stone Guest comes to dinner, the Don accepts him calmly, and promises to join the statue at his home for dinner the next night. Finally, Don Juan retreats into a fixed position of stylish hypocrisy in which he hopes to dupe his father and Donna Elvire's brother. Don Juan is resolute in his defiance and disbelief in the supernatural, and, implacable, he follows the statue into Hell as stage-flames consume him.

Don Juan mocks and exploits and warps moral principles throughout the play; and courage, love, faith, filial devotion, and honor are all distorted or beaten by Don Juan on his own terms. Moliere also seemed to think, at this point in his career, that mankind was quite vulnerable to such attacks.

DON JUAN
SGANARELLE—ACT I, SCENE I

PLAYER: MALE   AGE: ANY

Don Juan has married Donna Elvire so he could bed her. Once the conquest was made, he deserted her. He and Sganarelle have traveled seperately to Sicily, where Sganarelle awaits his first meeting with his master. While waiting, he is accosted by Guzman, one of Donna Elvire's servants, who has been traveling with her, searching for the Don. Guzman is irate at the actions of Don Juan and he cannot understand how a man could be so base and not honor his commitments to Donna Elvire. But Sganarelle knows, only too well.

SGANARELLE

[To GUZMAN.]
Ah! My poor Guzman, my good friend, you don't know yet, believe me, what sort of man Don Juan is. [...] If you knew the man as I do, you would not find it hard to believe that he left Donna Elvire. I cannot say for certain, of course, that he has changed towards her: I have no proof one way or the other as of yet. You know that he ordered me to come here before him, and we have not talked since his arrival. But as a warning, I tell you, between us, that in Don Juan, my master, you see one of the greatest scoundrels that ever walked the earth. He is a madman, a dog, a demon, a Turk, a heretic who doesn't believe in Heaven, Hell, saints, God, nor the Devil. He spends his life as a regular brute, an Epicurean swine; a true Sardanapalus, who goes deaf whenever you begin admonitions against him. He laughs at everything we believe in. You say that he married your mistress. Believe me, in order to satisfy his lust he would have married not only her, but you, her dog and her cat as part of the bargain. Marriage is nothing to him: it is a grand ruse he uses to

catch the fairer sex. And he will marry all comers wholesale: gentle-women, young girls, middle-class women, peasant girls—nothing escapes his notice. And if I were to list all the names of those he has married in different places, the recitation would last until midnight. You look surprised, and your color pales. Yet this is the mere outline of the man. To finish the portrait would require many more vigorous brush strokes. Let it be that the wrath of Heaven will some day deal with him. He cannot escape it. And at that time it would be better for me to owe my soul to the Devil than to still be this man. I have witnessed so much evil that I could wish him—I don't know where. But if a great lord is a wicked man, it is a terrible thing. I must be loyal to him, whatever I may think. Fear takes the place of loyalty in me, curbs my feelings, and often forces me to applaud that which I most detest.—Wait. He's coming, to take a walk in this place. Let us part. But listen: I have told you this in all confidence, and it fell rather quickly from my tongue. Yet if anything of what I have said to you should reach his ears, I will stoutly declare you a liar.

DON JUAN
DON JUAN—ACT I, SCENE 2

PLAYER: MALE   AGE: ANY

Don Juan has confessed to Sganarelle that a "new beauty has driven all thoughts of Donna Elvire" from his mind. This confirms only what Sganarelle had already suspected. When the servant starts to express his opinion, he stops, for fear of master-servant reprisals. When Don Juan gives his valet permission to say his mind, Sganarelle admits that he frankly does not approve of the Don's actions, and that it is "very wrong of you to make love right and left, as you do." Don Juan scoffs at Sganarelle's stance and in a cavalier manner states his position on the subject.

DON JUAN

[To SGANARELLE.]
What's this? Would you have a man bind himself to the first girl he falls in love with, to give up the world for her, and to have eyes for no one but her? A fine thing to be sure, to pride yourself on some false honor of fidelity, to lose yourself in one passion forever, and to be blinded from your youth to all other beautiful women! No, no: constancy is only for fools. Every beautiful woman has the right to charm us, and the woman who has the advantage of being the first one we meet should not deprive other women of their just claims over our hearts. As for me, I am delighted by beauty wherever I meet it, and I am easily overcome by the sweet violence with which it sweeps us along. It doesn't matter if I'm already engaged; the love I have toward one so fair does not bind me to do injustice to all the others; my eyes still see the merit in them all, and I pay the homage and tribute that Nature demands of us. Whatever may have happened before, I cannot refuse my love to any beautiful woman I behold. I would give away ten thousand hearts, if I had them, as soon as a fair face asks it of me. Besides, the first stirrings of love have indescribable charms, and the true pleasure of love consists in its variety. It's a delightful adventure to overcome by a hundred means the heart of a young beauty; to see day by day the progress you make; to shrink with sweet words, tears, and sighs the innocent modesty of a heart which is unwilling to yield; and to combat, inch by inch, all the little obstacles she places in the path of our passions; to overcome the scruples in which she places so much honor; and to lead her, step by step, to where we always intended to lead her. But, once we have won, there is nothing left to wish for; there is nothing more to say. All attraction of love is over, the passion becomes so tame that we fall asleep at the thought, unless some new object comes into our vision who awakens our desires and presents us with a new conquest then to be made. In short, there is no pleasure more wonderful than triumphing over the resistance of a beautiful woman. In this matter, I have the ambitions of a conqueror, who flies from victory to victory, and who cannot bring himself to put limits on his hunger. There is nothing that

can control my impetuous desires. I have a heart big enough for me to love the whole world, and, like Alexander, I could wish for other worlds to conquer as well.

DON JUAN
DONNA ELVIRE—ACT I, SCENE 3

PLAYER: FEMALE   AGE: ANY

Donna Elvire, a gracious and good lady, of romantic and trusting nature, with a convent education, met and fell for Don Juan. He spirited her away from her home, wed her in a ceremony he now mocks, and bedded her. Once done, he lost interest. She has followed him, hoping that what she fears is not true: that he is done with her. This is her first encounter with him in the play, and the first time she has seen him since he deserted her.

DONNA ELVIRE

[To DON JUAN and SGANARELLE.]
Will you do me the favor, Don Juan, of recognizing me? And may I hope, at least, that you will deign to turn your eyes this way? [...] Yes, I can see that you weren't expecting me, and you are surprised to see me, but in quite a different way than I had hoped. It proves to me what I altogether refused to believe. I wonder at my own simplicity and at my own weakness of heart in doubting a betrayal which is so confirmed by appearance. I have been kind enough, or rather I should say foolish enough, to try to deceive myself and to struggle to make a lie of what my eyes witnessed and my judgement concluded. My own tenderness manufactured reasons to excuse your growing coldness toward me, and I created a hundred excuses for your hasty departure, and to justify you for a crime which my common sense accused you. Day after day, I refused in vain to listen to my well-founded suspicions; I was deaf to their warning voices that make you guilty before me. I cherished

instead a thousand foolish fancies in my heart that strove to find you innocent, for that is what I wanted to believe. But all of that is over: your reception makes doubt no longer possible. The look you gave me when I greeted you told me much more than I ever wanted to know. However, I would like to hear in your own words why you left. Speak, Don Juan, I pray you, and let me hear how you will justify your actions.

DON JUAN
DONNA ELVIRE—ACT I, SCENE 3

PLAYER: FEMALE   AGE: ANY

Don Juan mocks Donna Elvire by refusing to speak to her directly, but speaks through Sganarelle, ordering him to explain their departure to the woman. Sganarelle, as any servant would who is caught in the middle, and in a situation in which he disapproves of the actions of his master to begin with, stumbles over an explanation. Rather than inhibit Donna Elvire, these actions simply makes her stronger in her resolve.

DONNA ELVIRE

Fie! How poorly you defend yourself, you a courtier who should be used to this sort of thing. I really pity you, the confusion you are in. Why don't you assume a noble's effrontery? Why don't you swear your feelings for me are unchanged? That you love me still with an unequalled love, and that nothing can ever part us? Why don't you say that business of greatest urgency forced you to leave me without the time to say goodbye; that in spite of your wishes you have to remain here for a time, and that the best thing I could do would be to return home, with the assurance that you will follow me as soon as possible—assured that you still burn for me and long to be with me again, that to be separated from me is to suffer the tortures of the body separated from its soul? This is how you should defend yourself, instead of standing there tongue-tied as you do!

DON JUAN
DONNA ELVIRE—ACT I, SCENE 3

PLAYER: FEMALE   AGE: ANY

When Don Juan is finally forced to address Donna Elvire, he "confesses" that he is a man of "scruples" and felt that he had forced her from the convent and that he could no longer live with her "in sin." He tells her that he felt he made her break her vows, and that he was seized with "repentance" and that he "dreaded the wrath of Heaven." He feared, he says, that their marriage was but "disguised adultery" and that it was his duty to leave her and try to forget her so that she could return to the convent and avoid the vengeance of Heaven falling on her head. That kind of rationalization is the last thing a woman betrayed wants to hear.

DONNA ELVIRE

O, villian! Now I really understand you, but to my misfortune it is too late, and my knowledge can only drive me to despair. But know this: your crime will not go unpunished. The very same Heaven that you mock will avenge me for your perfidy. [...] Enough! I will hear no more. I even chide myself for having heard too much already. It is despicable to have one's shame thrown back in one's face so clearly. When such a thing happens, the noble heart should know what to do at once. Do not fear: I will not rail against you with reproaches and insults— no, my anger will not dissipate itself only in empty words—I reserve all of its power for revenge. I repeat it once more: Heaven will punish you for your crimes against me. And if Heaven holds no terror for you, fear then, at least, the anger of an injured woman! *[Exit.]*

DON JUAN
SGANARELLE— ACT III, SCENE 1

PLAYER: MALE   AGE: ANY

Sganarelle's and Don Juan's adventures have lead them to a forest where they are both in disguise: Juan as a country gentleman, and Sganarelle as a doctor. They are both avoiding Don Juan's past catching up with them (i. e., Donna Elvire's brothers). Sganarelle says that his disguise as a doctor makes him feel "quite clever" and he wants to "argue" with Don Juan. About what, the Don wonders. On what you really believe, replies Sganarelle. Do you really believe in Heaven, or in Hell, or in anything on the earth? In reply, Don Juan answers that he believes two and two make four.

SGANARELLE

[To DON JUAN.]
You believe that "two and two make four, Sganarelle, and four and four make eight." A noble set of beliefs and grand articles of faith! Your religion, I see, is simple arithmetic. People get the strangest follies in their heads, and we must admit that some people are not always the wisest just because they have studied a lot. I have not studied like you, sir, thank God, and there is no one who can boast of ever having taught me anything; but with my own small kernel of common sense and my own little seed of judgment, I see things better than all the books can teach, and I know perfectly well that this world we see did not pop up overnight, like a mushroom. I ask you: who makes these trees, these rocks, this earth, this sky above us? Or did all of this spring up by itself? Here, for instance, are you: did you make yourself by yourself? Didn't your father have to know your mother for you to come into this world? Can you ever think of all the components that make up this machine called Man without marvelling at how one part connects with another? These nerves, these bones, these veins, these arteries, these—these lungs, this heart, this liver, and all the other ingredients found there, and which—Oh, please! Do stop me, do interrupt me, I can't argue

41

unless I'm interrupted. You remain silent on purpose, and let me go on talking out of pure spite. […] My argument, whatever you may think, is that there is something wonderful in man, which all of your scholars cannot explain. Isn't it astonishing that I am here and that I have in my head something which thinks a hundred different things a moment, and commands my body to do whatever it likes? I want to clap my hands, raise my arm, turn my eyes towards Heaven, bow my head, move my feet, go to the right, or to the left, forwards, backwards, turn—

[He turns and falls down while turning.]

Oh, fie! I am the world's prize fool to waste my time arguing with you. Believe what you like; what does it matter to me if you are damned or not!

DON JUAN
DONNA ELVIRE— ACT IV, SCENE 9

PLAYER: FEMALE   AGE: ANY

It is the night the Statue comes to dine with Don Juan. But first he has other visitors. He has just bilked a tradesman out of his money, and he mocks the admonitions given to him by his father. Then Donna Elvire arrives, quite unexpected and quite changed. She is veiled and disturbingly calm. She has come one last time to plead with Don Juan to amend his ways before the wrath of Heaven pours down upon his head.

DONNA ELVIRE

[She enters, veiled, speaks to DON JUAN, who is with SGANARELLE.]

Don't be surprised, Don Juan, to see me at this late hour and dressed like this. It is an urgent motive which brings me to you, and what I have to say cannot be delayed. I do not come here full of the wrath with which I left you this morning. I have changed greatly today. I am no longer that Donna Elvire who called for the vengeance of Heaven to rain upon you, and who

42

thought of nothing but threats and revenge. Heaven has relieved my soul of all of the unworthy passion I had for you; of all of those tumultuous excesses of a sinful infatuation; of all of those shameful demonstrations of a crude and earth-bound passion. Nothing remains in my heart but a love free of all sensual feelings; a holy tenderness; a love that craves for nothing, which no longer acts only for itself, and which cares only for what is best for you. [...] It is a pure and perfect love that brings me to you for your own good, to tell you of Heaven's warning, and to try to call you back from that chasm toward which you now run. Yes, Don Juan, I know of all the sins of your life; and that same Heaven which has touched my heart, and turned my eyes to my own errors, has inspired me to come and find you, to tell you that your cup of sins in Heaven is full, there is no mercy left, and that the wrath of Heaven is ready to fall on you. Only a prompt repentance can save you; you have one day, perhaps, to save yourself from the greatest of all miseries. I am no longer bound to you by any earthly ties. I thank Heaven that I have forsworn all of my worldly thoughts. I shall retreat into a convent, and once there ask only for enough time to expiate my sins, and to earn, by austere penitence, forgiveness for the blindness into which I was immersed through the ardor of a guilty passion. It would be an extreme sorrow to me, in my seclusion, to think that one person whom I cherished with such tenderness, had become a fearful example of Heaven's justice. But my joy would be unbounded if I could persuade you to avert the terrible fate which hangs above your head. Don Juan, as one last favor, grant me this sweet consolation. Do not refuse me your salvation, which I ask of you in tears. And if you are not moved by your own welfare, let yourself be moved by my prayers, and spare me the cruelty of knowing that you are condemned to eternal torments. [...] I loved you once with an extreme tenderness; nothing in this world was dearer to me than you were; I forgot all my duties for your sake; I have done everything for you; and all I ask in return is that you reform your life and escape eternal ruin. Save yourself, I beg you, if not for your own sake, then for mine. Once more, Don Juan, I ask it of you in tears. And if the tears of a woman you have loved are not enough, then I ask it of you in the name of whatever it is you do hold most dear. […] I will leave you now. This is all I had to say. […] Do not let us waste time in pointless words. Let me go away quickly. Do not trouble yourself with showing me out. Think only of taking my advice.

DON JUAN
DON JUAN—ACT V, SCENE 2

PLAYER: MALE   AGE: ANY

Here is the speech from Act V of DON JUAN in which Moliere attacked those who attacked his plays. Don Juan has just played an obsequious scene with his father, assuring the old man that he has amended his ways and is a reformed son. As soon as the old man has gone, Don Juan turns on Sganarelle, who has exuberantly congratulated Don Juan for seeing the light and have converted his ways. But lo! rather than having converted, Don Juan has dug his heels more solidly into his fixed position and is determined to use his "stylish vice" to his best advantages.

DON JUAN

[To SGANARELLE.]
A plague take that booby! Fie! You take as true account what I have just said, and you believe my lips agree with my heart? […] Oh, dear no. I am not changed at all, and my thoughts are still the same. […] There is certainly something about a statue moving and speaking which I do not understand; but whatever it may be, it is neither capable of convincing my mind nor of staggering my soul. And if I said I wanted to reform and to lead an exemplary life, it is done out of pure expediency, a useful deception, a necessary distortion, to which I submit willingly, in order to appease a father I need, and to safeguard myself, in the eyes of mankind, against a hundred troublesome adventures in which I may become entangled. I gladly make you my confidant in this business, Sganarelle, because I very much want one

witness to my innermost feelings and as to the real motives that
oblige me to act as I do. [...] After all, there are plenty of others
besides me who wear the same feathers, and who make use of
the same mask to deceive the world. [...] There is no longer any
shame in hypocrisy. It is a fashionable vice, and all fashionable
vices pass for virtues. The role of a good man is the best part
one can act. The professional hypocrite has wonderful
advantages. The art of imposture enjoys wide-spread respect
today; and even if the world uncovers the deceit, it says nothing
against it. All of man's other vices are susceptible to censure,
and everyone is at liberty to attack and expose them boldly. But
hypocrisy is a privileged vice, whose fist closes over the mouth
of everyone and in peace enjoys a sovereign impunity. A league
is formed with others, each of whom recognizes in others the
same language and attitudes. If one of the league is offended, the
culprit draws the whole pack down on his back; and while those
whom we know to be sincere and who are known to have acted
in good faith, are always, I say, the dupes of others. They are
caught in the web of the hypocrites and blindly lend their
support to those who only ape their genuine conduct. You
wouldn't believe the number of people I know, who, with the
help of such a stratagem, have put but new costumes on their
disordered youths, have sought shelter in the cloak of piety, and
in its venerated robes are allowed to be as wicked as they please.
It doesn't matter that people are aware of their intrigues, and
know them for what they are, their esteem in society is no less
real. They are well received everywhere. They bow their heads,
exhale a mortified sigh, expound regret with an emotional sob,
roll their eyes to Heaven a time or two, and lo and behold! all is
forgiven. It is under these convenient robes that I mean to take
shelter and put my affairs to rights. I shall not desert my dear
habits, but I will carefully conceal them; I will avoid all noise
about my pleasures. If I am discovered, the whole cabal will
take up my interest of their own accord, and they will defend me
against the whole world. In short, it is the safest way for me to
do exactly as I want with impunity. I shall set myself up as a
censor of other people's actions. I shall judge everyone as evil,
and speak good about no one but myself. If I am even slightly
offended, I shall never forgive, but shall retain always an

irreconcilable hatred. I shall play the avenger of Heaven, and under this appropriate disguise, I will harass my enemies. I will accuse them of impieties. I will contrive to set those zealous gossips who, without knowing nor understanding anything, let alone the truth, to attacking my foes in public, and to damn them with no more authority than that which they award to themselves. It is this way that we can profit by the weakness of other men; and it is this way that an intelligent man can accommodate himself to the vices of his age.

∞∞

THE MISANTHROPE
[Le Misanthrope]

THE MISANTHROPE has been referred to as Moliere's darkest comedy of manners on humanity, as his possible "masterpiece," and has been regarded as "Moliere's HAMLET." It is all these things—and perhaps a lot more. It comes at the end of the creative period that produced TARTUFFE and DON JUAN. And in these three great plays of the mid-1660s, Moliere is clearly testing the limits of comedy. (It is also interesting to note that after the composition of THE MISANTHROPE and its two sister plays, Moliere's remaining works were bright and bubbly. It is almost as if he had learned through the purgatory of the composition of these three plays how he could now say all the dark things about man he had to say in dazzling sunlight, no matter how grotesque were the subjects or the traits of his characters.) THE MISANTHROPE is a masterpiece. In it, Moliere not only illustrates the absurdities and manners of his time, but he also depicts the weaknesses of the human heart. And that portrait belongs to all ages.

And THE MISANTHROPE is a comedy, and a comedy about virtue. Alceste is a comic, not a tragic hero, as Moliere resoundingly assures us in the opening scene of the play. Alceste is a man of sterling integrity and a man who's standards of virtues are so rigid they may never be able to bend to this world. Alceste is so excessive in his pursuit of the "truth" that he has become embittered over the superficiality of society and is thinking of withdrawing from the "civilized world." As Moliere establishes in the opening scene of the play, it may be honorable to protest the proliferation of "white lies" in one's social life; but it is comic to urge *suicide* as the only atonement for such a "crime," as Alceste urges on his friend, Philante. This is a comedy—not a farce—but a comedy of manners, deeply rooted in the absurdities and foibles of a ritualized society.

The play was not a resounding success when it was first produced. It opened on June 4, 1666, and it was withdrawn approximately two months later in favor of THE DOCTOR IN SPITE OF HIMSELF. During Moliere's career, the play did but a few performances a year. But time has supported the play, and now THE MISANTHROPE has been recognized as the great play it is. If it is known better in the library than it is on the stage, that is because it is an extremely difficult play to conquer as an actor.

Alceste is in love with Celimene, who is very much a part of the society he despises. She is a flirt, and she very much enjoys baiting men with the affections she shows them, then pitting them against one another. Celimene is finally exposed when two letters to two of her paramours are revealed, though the machinations of Arsinoe, one of Cleimene's social rivals. Alceste will forgive her if she will agree to retire from the world with him, but she refuses. Alceste does depart at the end of the play, alone, more violently determined than ever to flee from this world and find peace where "one can be free to be a man of honor."

THE MISANTHROPE
ALCESTE—ACT II SCENE 1

PLAYER: MALE   AGE: ANY

The ways of love are strange—as Moliere has shown us in previous plays—so it is not shocking that Alceste would assume aspects of intractable misanthropy while trying to win Celimene. Alceste truly loves the flirtatious widow, for as he says late in the play, he lost his judgment and took "the poison, which is killing me" when he saw her (poison being a metaphor for the hypocritical aspects of society). Act II opens with a conversation between Alceste and Celimene. He tries his power tactics on her. The last thing he wants is to lose her. Celimene, for her part, wants to keep Alceste among her string of admirers.

ALCESTE

Madam, shall I be frank with you? I am far from satisfied with your behavior; I am much grieved because of it, and I think we shall have to part. Yes, I would deceive you were I to speak otherwise. Sooner or later a rupture would inevitably occur, and even if I promised a thousand times to the contrary, it would not be within my power to prevent it. [...] I do not scold, madam, but your heart is too easily opened to all first-comers. I see too many lovers laying siege to you, and my heart cannot witness this without pain. [...] No, madam, it is not a stick you want to drive them away, but a heart less ready to yield to their love-tales. That your beauty travels with you wherever you go, I know; but the reception you give them keeps near you all those whom your eyes have attracted; and the gentleness you show to those you have conquered, in every case, completes the work begun by your charms. The stimulated hopes you inspire in your admirers just fuels their persevering around you, whereas if just once or twice you would staunchly discourage them, the whole crowd might go away. Will you tell me, at least, madam, what your Clitandre possesses that pleases you so much? Is it the long nail on his little finger that has won your affectionate regard? Do you surrender, along with the whole of the fashion world, to the shining merits of his periwig? Do you love him because of his canions—his stiffly starched linens adorned with lace that dance below his knees—to those does he owe your love for him? Or, perhaps, his great collection of ribbons have the powers to charm you? Don't tell me it's the attraction of his bellowing German breeches, tied with the ribbons around his knees, that has gained for him you heart, while all the time he is calling himself your slave. Perhaps it is his laughter or his practiced falsetto voice that are his secret keys to unlocking your heart. Fie! Forget about his help with your lawsuit. Lose your lawsuit with all the courage you can, and don't humor a rival who is offensive to me.

THE MISANTHROPE
ARSIONE—ACT III, SCENE 5

PLAYER: FEMALE   AGE: ANY

One of the great cat fights in comedic theatre occurs in Act III of this play between Celimene and one of her social rivals, Arsione. Shortly before her entrance, Celimene and her entourage have taken Arsione to task for her prudishness, her ardent zeal, and her anxiety to snare a lover. Arsione and Celimene are not friends, but they are not quite enemies, either—yet. But both women do understand the rituals and conventions of the polite society of their times. They converse with each each other not so much in direct statements as in an elaborate code, which is recognized and deciphered by everyone who listens. Arsione has just been announced, which miffs Celimene, yet she greets Arsione with all the social cordiality required. Arsione, for her part, comes directly to the point of her visit—such urgency it is for the welfare of Celimene.

ARSIONE

[To CELIMENE.]
True friendship, madam, ought to show especially in those things which are of greatest importance to us. And as there are no matters of more consequence than honor and reputation in society, I've come to prove my friendship for you by bringing you information on something which closely touches upon your honor. Yesterday I visited some virtuous and distinguished friends, and the conversation turned, by chance, madam, to you. I am sorry to say that your behavior and the scandal it causes was far from meeting approval. Your visitors, your coquettish conduct, and the rumors which arise from it, aroused excessive censors more numerous than expected, and criticism so severe that I was quite distressed by it. You can easily imagine, I am sure, whose part I took. I did everything in my power to defend you. In my plea for you, I insisted your conduct was based on your good intentions, and I even vouched for the integrity of your heart. But you know that in this life there are certain things

49

we cannot excuse, no matter how hard we try to do so. And I was forced, at last, to acknowledge that the manner of your life does reflect on your reputation. The way you entertain does cause the world to wonder, and not to the good, and you do give rise to regrettable gossip being spread about. If you would but amend your ways, your whole conduct might offer fewer occasions for the use of less charitable tongues. Not that I would believe for a moment that your virtue has been impuned: Heaven preserve me from such a thought! But people too easily presume guilt, and it is not sufficient to lead a blameless life for ourselves if we neglect its appearances as well. You are too sensible, madam, I know, not to take this advice in the way that it is meant, and to recognize that I am prompted only by my affection for you and my zeal for your best welfare.

THE MISANTHROPE
CELIMENE—ACT III, SCENE 5

PLAYER: FEMALE   AGE: ANY

This is Celimene's immediate reply to Arsione's reportage of reaction to Celimene's conduct and the proffering of her advise as how to stem wagging tongues and amend her ways. Celimene does not let anyone in society, especially another female, get the better of her.

CELIMENE

[To ARSIONE.]
Madam, I am deeply grateful to you, and such advise as you proffer makes me much obliged to you. Far from taking it unkindly, I would at once like to show my appreciation by telling you something which itself touches on your own reputation. As I see you show your friendship for me by reporting the tales others circulate about me, I'll take your kind display as my example and acquaint you with what people say about you. I visited friends at their home the other day, and there

I met a group of people with the most extraordinary merit. They spoke of the duties of a virtuous life, and the conversation, madam, turned to you. Your prudishness and inordinate zeal were by no means cited as the best of all possible models. Your affectation of a grave demeanor; your everlasting declamations on discretion and honor; your simpering and your clamoring at the least hint of impropriety which the most ambiguous innocent word may present. You hold yourself in such high esteem, and cast piteous looks on all those around you; your frequent and sharp criticisms of things that are harmless and pure. All of this, madam, if I may be frank, was by common accord, condemned. "Why does she," they asked, "assume a modest bearing and a sagacious manner, which is a strange contrast to her actions? She is exact in her time to pray, but she beats her servants and refuses to pay them their wages. She makes the greatest display of piety in church or shrine, by why then does she paint her face and always strive to be a beauty? She has all nudes in the paintings in her house clothed, yet she delights in the real thing itself." For my part, I came to your defense in face of them all. I assured them all it was slander, but they would do nothing but criticize. The conclusion was that you would do well to be less solicitous about the acts of others and to look a little more closely at your own. We should do a great deal of self-examination before we begin admonishing others. We ourselves should lead an exemplary life before we pretend to make corrections in our neighbors; and that we leave this task better still to those whom Heaven has ordained. Madam, I, too, believe that you are also too sensible not to take this advise in the way it is meant, and to recognize that it is prompted by my affection for you and my zeal for your best welfare.

THE MISANTHROPE
ALCESTE—ACT IV, SCENE 3

PLAYER: MALE   AGE: ANY

Arsione wants a lover, and Alceste is just as good a candidate as any other—perhaps even a shade better, all things considered. Arsione has tried all of her powers of persuasion to turn Alceste's head toward her and away from Celimene. She has tried by indicating she will use her influence at Court to further Alceste's own position there; then she assumes the role of the sympathetic friend who must perform the painful duty of telling him that his love for Celimene has been betrayed. She takes Alceste to her house where she shows him two letters Celimene has written to other admirers. Alceste has just returned from reading the letters and to confront Celimene with her infidelity.

ALCESTE

[Aside.]
O, Heaven! Help me master my anger!
[To CELIMENE.]
All of the wickedness of which a soul is capable, nothing is comparable to your perfidy. The worst of Fates, the Devils and vengeful Heaven can do has never produced anything as faithless as you. [...] No! No more jests, this is not a time for laughter. You should blush with shame; you have ample reason to do so: your treachery is proved. The apprehension I felt in my heart has proved right. My perceptions were too well founded, and my frequent suspicions, which you thought odious and unsound, were true guides. I followed their paths and with my own eyes uncovered your chicanery. Yes, in spite of all your caution and all of your skill at duplicity, I have discovered the truth about you. And don't think you can play me for the fool, or that I shall bear this insult unavenged. I know that we have no power to govern our desires; that love is always spontaneous; that we cannot possess a heart by force, and that every heart must name its own master. I would have no complaint, if you had rejected my overtures outright from the very first, Celimene,

and had spoken truly to me without dissemblance. Even though you would have crushed me to the wellspring of my life, I should have blamed nothing but my ill-lighted stars for it. But you encouraged my love! For such treachery, for such perfidy, no punishment seems too great. And I shall give full vent to my vexation. After perpetrating such an outrage, fear everything from me, Celimene. I am no longer master of myself: anger has conquered me. I am pierced to the heart by the cruel shaft you have let fly to kill me. My senses are no longer governed by reason. I yield myself over to a just revenge. I cannot answer for what I may do.

THE MISANTHROPE
CELIMENE—ACT IV, SCENE 3

PLAYER: FEMALE   AGE: ANY

A great deal of Celimene's sustenance comes from her string of admirers and her ability to convince each one of them that he has a special place in her heart. But enough is enough. Alceste mounts accusation upon accusation and when he demands she present proof that the letter is "innocent," and that she strive to appear "faithful" to him, and he will "strive" to believe her, Celimene draws the line. There comes a moment in every relationship in which the demands of compromise cause one party to give more to the other than will be received in return.

CELIMENE

[To ALCESTE.]
Believe me! You are a fool with your jealous fits. Leave me. You don't deserve the love I have for you. Whatever makes you think I would stoop to condescend to the baseness of pretending for your sake, or that if I were in love with another man I would not frankly tell you so? Does not the fact that I give you my assurance of my feelings for you serve as an answer against your suspicions? And is not my own word some defense against

them? You insult me when you give way to your fears. And since we women require a great effort to confess our love, and since a woman's honor is the adversary of love and it so strictly forbids such a confession, should not the man, when he has seen a woman surmount all these obstacles to make such a revelation, think so lightly of that testimony? He should know our word is not to be discounted. Is a man not guilty if he does not trust what we have spoken only after so much inner conflict and with subdued reluctance? Indeed, my fury should be the reward for such incertitudes. You do not deserve my care and consideration. O! I am a fool myself and I am vexed at my own simpleness that I still have some regard for you. I ought to find someone else to show my affections and give you a proper reason for complaint.

THE MISANTHROPE
ALCESTE—ACT V, SCENE 1

PLAYER: MALE   AGE: ANY

Alceste has reached the nadir of his disillusionment with humanity. The reversal of his fortunes on all fronts and Fate's blows on his back he has experienced during the time span of the play have done nothing to deter his opinion that mankind ranks somewhere on the scales of the universe with that of a colony of maggots on a dunghill. Besides his "betrayal" by Celimene, Alceste has just lost an important lawsuit in the courts due to perjured testimony. Alceste is adamant about retreating from society totally and living in the wilderness, and he is deaf to all reasoning.

ALCESTE

[To PHILANTE.]
It's no use, I tell you. My decision is made. [...] You can wheedle and coax and argue until you are blue in the face, but it will all be in vain. Nothing you can say will make me change my

plans. Too much perversity reigns in our age and I am resolved to avoid all further dealings with the society of men. Look at what has happened to me! Honor, probity, decency, virtue, and the laws were on my side, men published in papers the justice of my cause, and I put my trust in right and equity. Yet in the end, I am defeated! I have justice on my side, and I lose my case! A miserable scoundrel, whose shameful history is written on his face for everyone to read, perjures himself with the blackest lie, and he wins triumphantly. All good faith acceeds before his treachery. He cuts my throat and blames me for it. He aims his artificial, hypocritical gaze at the judge, and all justice kneels to his sway. He gets a decree from the court to crown his infamy; and not satisfied with the injury already done to me, he proclaims that the authorship of a tract now in circulation—a pamphlet so abominable that the mere reading of it should be banned by law!—he subscribes the authorship of that tract to me! Where upon, Oronte is seen to nod his head in ascent and seconds the calumny! Oronte, who is said to be an honorable man, and to whom I have done no other wrong but to have been honest with him; Oronte, who comes to me though I advised him against it, eagerly asks my opinion of the verses he writes. And because I tell him frankly what I think, and betray neither him nor the truth, he helps to crush me as he attests to a crime that never existed. He becomes my greatest enemy, and will never forgive me, because I could not pronounce his poem good. By Heaven above, this is what all men are like. The itch for glory leads them to commit such actions. Yes: this is the good faith, the virtuous zeal, the justice, and the honor we find in men revealed. No: it its too much to endure the sorrows caused by their malice. I have endured enough of men. Come, let us flee these ugly woods, let us escape this cut-throat place. And since men behave like wolves, these traitors shall not see my face again. I bid them my last farewell.

THE MISER
[L'Avare]

Harpagon, the miser of the title of this play, has as dark a heart, is as dementedly obsessed, and is as absurdly aberrated as any character Moliere created for his darkest plays. Harpagon's human spirit has been corrupted by his lust for gold. Yet because of his mastery of comic technique and farce, Moliere is able to take one of the meanest of human foibles and make an audience howl with pleasure at its grotesqueness. Moliere takes the themes of money and greed, sex and power, and the dysfunctional family—all potential material of the great moral drama—and turns them into a work of comedic art.

The Parisian public saw THE MISER for the first time on September 9, 1668, and it was a success almost from the beginning. Moliere played Harpagon, a character so obsessed with his money that the love if it takes the place of all natural affection. Harpagon not only withdraws from all family functions and discussions, from all family interest, he also considers his own children his natural enemies. Harpagon is the embodiment of the acquisition of money for acquisition's sake taken to the borders of sanity.

Harpagon is a widower with two grown children. The brother and sister, Cleante and Elise, fight to choose their own mates rather than have them chosen for them by their father, who will choose according to his parsimony. Harpagon plans to marry again—to a young girl named Marianne. Unknown to Harpagon, his own son is his rival for the girl's affections. And unknown to Cleante, his own father is the money lender who is charging outrageous interest (25%) on a loan so Cleante can leave home and marry Marianne. During the course of events, Cleante's servant, Le Fleche, learns where Harpagon hides his money box, and he steals it for Cleante. When Cleante forces Harpagon to choose between the money box and the girl, Harpagon chooses the money box. At the end, when young love once again is triumphant, and everyone else goes off to share their joy and celebrate their approaching marriages, Harpagon goes off to share his joy and celebrate with his money box, his "only friend."

THE MISER
LE FLECHE—ACT II, SCENE 5

PLAYER: MALE   AGE: ANY

Le Fleche is attached to Harpagon's household as
Cleante's valet. But there is no doubt that La Fleche only wears
the title because that is the job he was given. Le Fleche is one of
those servants who knows how to survive, who is loyal to his
master because he likes him, but stays with a job because he
needs one, or there is an advantage to be gained. There is also
some question as to the number of legitimate ventures Le Fleche
can boast about in his background. What is evident is that he
knows the back alleys and whom to watch to find out where the
treasure is buried—or the skeletons. At some time in his past he
has had dealings with Frosine, the matchmaker, for they seem to
know one another and are on friendly terms.

LE FLECHE

[To FROSINE.]
Aha! Is that you, Frosine? What are you doing here? [...] You
have business with the master of this house? [...] Ho! Ho! You
will have to be most clever to get any money out of this one. Let
me tell you, ready money is all but extinct in this house. [...] I
am your 'umble servant, but you as of yet do not know
Monsieur Harpagon. Of all human beings, Monsieur Harpagon
is the least humane human; of all mortals, he is the mortal that is
the hardest and has the tightest fist. There is no service great
enough to persuade him to open his purse. If you want praise,
esteem, a kind word, friendly good will, you are welcome to
take what you want. But money—there's another matter. There
is nothing more dry, nothing more fallow, than his favors and
his good graces, but he has such an aversion to the word
"give"—he never says "I give"—he even says "I *lend* you a
good morning. [...] All your talents are useless trifles here. I
defy you to soften up the man we speak about as far as money is
concerned. He is acrimonious where money is concerned, and
so malevolent it would drive anyone to despair. We might starve

to death right in front of him, and he wouldn't budge 'is little finger to buy groats. The short of it is, he loves money more than reputation, virtue and honor. The merest hint that anyone might ask him for something from his purse will cause him to go into convulsions. It's like striking him at the most vital spot on his body, it's like piercing his heart, it's like tearing out his very bowels! And if—but here he comes back. I'm off. I leave him to you.

THE MISER
FROSINE—ACT II, SCENE 6

PLAYER: FEMALE   AGE: ANY (MATURE)

Frosine is a woman of indeterminate age and of questionable background. But there is no questioning her many talents for intrigue, thinking fast on her feet, and surviving. She is at present in the business of being a matchmaker who has a talent, too, for panegyrics on the charms of old people. She has to make matches between disparate people work because she doesn't get her commission if she doesn't. Her biggest challenge right now is to get the Miser to accept a girl who has no dowry and to convince him that he's getting a bargain in the bride.

FROSINE

[To HARPAGON.]
She is a girl who will bring you twelve thousand francs a year. Is that nothing? [...] To begin with, she has been raised and trained with the strictest precepts of frugality. She is a girl accustomed to live on salad, milk, cheese, and apples, so consequently she will require no well-served table, nor elegant consume´s, nor your ceaseless broth of peeled barley; in short, none of those delicacies that another woman would desire. This is no small matter, and may well amount to three thousand francs annually. Furthermore, she only cares for simplicity and

neatness. She will have nothing to do with expensive, splendid dresses nor rich jewels, or none of those sumptuous furnishings that other girls her age indulge in with such extravagance. This in itself is worth more than four thousand francs per year. Finally, she has the strongest aversion to gambling, and this is not very common among women today. Why, I know that one of my neighbor women lost twenty thousand francs in gambling this year. But let's take only a quarter of that amount. Five thousand francs a year at gambling and four thousand in dresses and jewels makes nine thousand, and if you add the other three thousand which we counted for food, does that not make twelve thousand francs a year?

THE MISER
MASTER JACQUES—ACT III, SCENE 5

PLAYER: MALE   AGE: ANY

Master Jacques is the servant in the house who assumes a number of jobs, and right now he is Harpagon's coachman and his cook. Whenever Master Jacques talks to Harpagon, in whatever capacity, he changes his hat—still the universal symbol of multiple jobs. Master Jacques also seems to be the only one of the household servants who will confront Harpagon with the truth about his reputation in the city and among the citizens.

MASTER JACQUES

[To HARPAGON.]
Since you insist it, Monsieur, I will tell you frankly that you are the laughing stock of the whole city. We are taunted everywhere by a thousand jokes on your account. Nothing delights other citizens more than to make sport of you, and to tell stories upon stories upon stories—without end—about your stinginess. One man says that you have special almanacs printed in which you double the number of fast days and vigils so that you may make a profit from the fasts which you inflict upon all in your

59

household. Another man insists that you have ready-made quarrels for your servants at Christmastide, or when they leave your service, so that you don't have to give them anything. Still another gossips as how you prosecuted your neighbor's cat not long ago because it ate what was left of a leg of mutton. Another tells a story that one night you were caught stealing oats from your own horses' troff to use for your breakfast porridge—and being caught in the dark by your coachman—the man before me—he gave you a sound beating with a stick, and you have said nothing about it because you wanted no one to know. In short, what else is there for me to tell you? We can go no where but that we won't hear you torn to pieces and raked over the coals. No one ever speaks of you, nor mentions your name, without calling you a miser, stingy, mean, skinflint, pinchpenny, and a usurer.

THE MISER
FROSINE—ACT IV, SCENE 1

PLAYER: FEMALE   AGE: ANY (MATURE)

There is another side to Frosine: she is romantic. As soon as she learns that Marianne and Cleante are in love she begins scheming on how to dupe Harpagon and change his mind. She does this, quite frankly, because Harpagon is not a favorite client of hers, and she likes the young people. But at the same time, she is very aware that she must look to her own survival as well.

FROSINE

[With CLEANTE, MARIANNE, ELISE.]
It really is unfortunate that neither of you told me all about your involvement with each other before. I might certainly have done something to avert this trouble, and would not have let things go this far. [...] A rather difficult piece of business.
[To MARIANNE.]

As far as your mother is concerned, she is not altogether unreasonable, and we might win her over and persuade her to give to the son the gift she intended to give to the father.

[To CLEANTE.]

The biggest problem is your father. [...] I know he will bear malice if he is refused, and afterwards he will be in no way disposed to give consent to the marriage of the two of you. It would be better if we could make him refuse you, my child. Marianne, you have to find ways to make him dislike you. [...]

[Beat.]

Yes: right enough, no doubt. That is what ought to be done. But how in the world are we going to go about it? Wait a moment. What if we had a woman of somewhat advanced years who had a little of the ability I possess, and who is able to impersonate a lady of rank, and with a retinue, which is assembled in haste, and with some fanciful title of marquise or viscountess, and whom we assume is from Lower Brittany? I have the skills to convince your father that she is a very rich woman—that besides a number of houses, she has a hundred thousand francs in ready money; that she is *deeply* in love with him, and that she would marry him at any cost, even if it were to surrender all her money to him by terms of the marriage contract. I have no doubt he would listen to that proposal. For while he certainly loves you, my dear Marianne, yet he loves money still more. And once seduced by the glitter of this allure, and has consented to your marriage, Cleante, to Marianne, it does not matter a peach pit how disillusioned he is by the truth about his passionate marquise.

THE MISER
HARPAGON—ACT IV, SCENE 7

PLAYER: MALE   AGE: MATURE

Disaster! Catastrophe! Destruction! The Big One has hit Harpagon's house. Harpagon has gone out to his garden for his every-ten-minute-check on his money box, and it is not there! Harpagon has been robbed! His property has been desecrated. Nothing else matters but that his money box be recovered. All other thoughts are driven from his mind. All other problems are infinitesimal by comparison. The cares of his family and their happiness are as noticeable as more water poured into a river in measure with this infamy!

HARPAGON

[Rushing in from the garden.]
Thieves! Thieves! Assassins! Murder! Justice, just Heaven! I am finished! I am murdered! They have cut my throat. They have stolen my money! Who can it be? What's become of him? Where is he? Where is he hiding? What shall I do to find him? Where shall I run? Where shall I not run? Is he not here? Or there? Who's this? Stay! Stop!
[He catches his own arm.]
Give me my money, you scoundrel—! Oh! It's me. My mind is jumbled, and I don't know where I am, who I am, or what I am doing. Alas! My poor money. My poor money! My dearest friend! They have deprived me of you; and since you are gone, I have lost my support, my consolation, my joy. All is finished for me, and there is nothing more for me to do in this world. It's impossible for me to live without you. Life is over; I can bear it no longer. I'm dying; I'm dead; I'm buried. Is there no one who will call me back from the grave, by restoring my dear money to me, or by telling me who stole it? Eh? Who said that? It's no one. Whoever committed this heinous crime must have watched diligently for this opportunity, and he must have chosen the very moment when I was talking with my miscreant of a son to do it. I must go. I'll demand justice. I'll have my whole household put

to torture—my maids, my serving men, my daughter, my son, myself as well!
[He looks at the audience.]
What crowd is this? Everyone of them looks like a thief to me. There is not one person out there that I don't suspect. Eh? What are they talking about over there? Is it about him that took my money? What noise is that up there? Is my thief among you up there? For the love of Heaven, if any of you know anything about my thief, I beg you to tell me. Is he hiding out there amongst you? They all look at me and laugh. You'll see: they are all involved and connected with this robbery. Come here, quick! Officers of the watch, provosts, magistrates, judges, racks, gibbets, and hangmen! I'll hang everybody in the world, and if I don't find my money, I'll hang myself afterwards.
[Exit.]

∞∞∞

THE IMAGINARY INVALID
[Le Malade Imaginaire]

THE IMAGINARY INVALID is the last play Moliere wrote. It premiered on February 10, 1673, and during its fourth performance a week later, on February 17, 1673, Moliere is stricken with a seizure during the performance, coughing up blood, but he manages to turn the episode into a part of the play. He collapses at the curtain, and is taken home where he dies an hour later. For years he had been suffering from lung and pulmonary disorders. It is assumed that during this performance blood vessels in his throat or lung burst, and the bleeding could not be halted. Moliere, a complete man of the theatre, and a man who scarificed everything for it, almost dies, literally, on the stage. Moliere's final play struck a fitting note. It is a farce about a hypochondriac who is intent upon achieving the illusion of health and vitality. Moliere was sick and near dying while writing this play, and many of the complaints and descriptions which Argan expresses are those which the fatally-ill playwright was suffering. Moliere's works offered the only illusions and vitality that would give him his only triumph over death—the immortality of a great dramatist.

Argan is a wealthy bourgeois who has become obsessed with his health and with illness as a way to fulfill his desire for attention and self-indulgence. His excessive hypochondria makes him the perfect target for the charlatans in the medical profession. And Beline, Argan's mercenary, second wife, hopes that the medical cures will kill him so she can inherit his fortune. To assure constant medical attention, Argan arranges for his daughter, Angelique, to marry the imbecilic Thomas Diafoirus, son of a pompous physician who spurns all new medical discoveries and "clings" to the superstitions of the "ancients." (The thick-headed Thomas will be made a doctor in three days.) Through the intervention of Toinette, Argan's cheeky maid, Beline's plot is revealed to Argan, and Angelique is allowed to marry the man she loves. Toinette also assumes the disguise of a 90-year-old physician and takes Argan's obsession to the extremes. The play ends with a mock ceremony investing Argan as a doctor, so he will always be able to attend to himself.

THE IMAGINARY INVALID
ARGAN—ACT I, SCENE 1

PLAYER: MALE   AGE: MATURE

This is the first scene in the play. Argan is alone on stage with his medical bills and his counter. It is the first introduction the audience has to his obsessions, his hypochondria, and his absurd foibles concerning both the need and payment of medical treatment.

ARGAN

[Sitting at a table, totalling his apothecary bills, with counters.]
Three and two make five, and five make ten, and ten makes twenty. Three and two make five. Item: on the twenty-fourth of the month, a small enema, insinuative, preparatory, and emollient, to soften, moisten, and refresh the entrails of

Monsieur Argan. What pleases me about Monsieur Fleurant, my apothecary, is that his bills are always polite: "Monsieur's entrails, thirty sous." Yes, but Monsieur Fleurant, it is not enough just to be polite, one must also be reasonable, and not fleece the sick. Thirty sous for an enema! I am your respectful servant, as I have already told you, but you have charged me in past bills only twenty sous for an enema, and twenty sous in the language of the apothecaries means ten sous. Here, then, are ten sous. Item: on the same day, a good detergent enema consisting of double catholicon, rhubarb, rose honey, and other ingredients, according to the prescription, to clean, scour, work, and to flush Monsieur's entrails, thirty sous. With your permission, ten sous. Item: on the evening of the same day, a hepatic, soporiferous, and somniferous julep prepared to induce sleep for Monsieur, thirty-five sous. I do not complain about that, for it made me sleep very well. Ten, fifteen and sixteen sous, six deniers. Item: on the twenty-fifth, a good purgative and corroborative mixture composed of fresh cassia, with Levantine senna, and other ingredients, according to the prescription of Monsieur Purgon, to expel Monsieur Argan's bile, four francs. Ah! Monsieur Fleurant, this must be a joke. You must learn to be reasonable with your patients. Monsieur Purgon never ordered you to put four francs. Make it three francs, if you please. Twenty and thirty sous. Item: on the same day, a potion of anodyne and an astringent to help Monsieur Argan to repose, thirty sous. Ten sous, Monsieur Fleurant. Good, ten and fifteen sous. Item: on the twenty-sixth, an carminative enema to allow Monsieur to pass wind, thirty sous. Item: the same enema repeated that same night, thirty sous. Monsieur Fleurant, ten sous. Item: on the twenty-seventh, an excellent mixture designed to drive out the ill-humours of Monsieur Argan, three francs. Good; twenty and thirty sous. I am glad you are reasonable. Item: on the twenty-eighth, a dose of clarified and sweetened whey, to soften, temper, purify and restore Monsieur Argan's blood, twenty sous. Good, we'll say ten sous. Item: a cordial and prescriptive potion, composed of a dozen grains of bezoar, syrup of lemon and pomegranates, and other ingredients, according to the prescription, five francs. Ah! Monsieur Fleurant, go gently, if you please! If you go on like that, no one will want to be sick anymore. Content yourself with four francs. Twenty and forty sous. Three and two are five, and five is ten, and ten is twenty. Sixty-three francs, four sous, and six deniers. So, during this month I have taken one, two, three, four, five, six, seven, eight mixtures; and one, two three, four, five, six, seven, eight, nine, ten, eleven, twelve enemas. And last month there were twelve mixtures and twenty enemas. I am not surprised, then, that I am not so well this month as last. I will speak to Monsieur Purgon about it, so he can put the matter right. Come take all of this away.

[He sees that he is alone.]

There's nobody here. There's no use talking; I'm always left alone. There is no way of keeping them here.

[He rings the hand bell to summon the servants.]

Ting-a-ling-a-ling. They don't hear, and this bell doesn't make enough noise.

[The bell again.]

Ting-a-ling-a-ling. No use.

[Rings again.]

They're all deaf! Toinette!

[Rings bell.]

Toinette! I'm growing angry. *Ting-a-ling-a-ling! Ting-a-ling-a-ling!* ` It's just as if I've not rung at all.

[Rings the bell with great fury and shouts at the top of his lungs.]

Toinette! You jade! You hussy! Come here at once!

[He ceases to ring the bell, but he cries out:]

Ding, Ding! Ding, Ding! O! This is pitiful. Ding, Ding! Ding, Ding!!—Oh, my God! They will leave me here to die! Toinette!

[He continues to ring and shout.]

Ding, Ding! Ding, Ding!! DING, DING!!!

ABOUT THE EDITOR

Dick Dotterer is the editor of SHAKESPEARE'S MONOLOGUES THEY HAVEN'T HEARD, and SHAKESPEARE'S MONOLOGUES FOR WOMEN also in this series. He has had 17 of his playscripts produced internationally and 5 of them have been published. He has also prepared English prose adaptations of Moliere's THE SCHOOL FOR HUSBANDS and SGANARELLE. He has directed 60 stage productions, worked in television, and winked at the movies. He has portrayed 79 different roles as an actor. He has also worked as a dramaturg and literary manager; and he has worked in educational theatre, taught acting, and guest lectured on playwriting, on directing, and on performing farce techniques. His experience with Moliere includes being associated with productions of THE SCHOOL FOR WIVES, THE DOCTOR IN SPITE OF HIMSELF, and THE IMAGINARY INVALID. He holds an M. F. A. in playwriting and directing.

ORDER DIRECT